The Birthing Process

ISBN: 978-0-615-62664-2

Copyright © 2012 Tapika M. Howard

All rights reserved. No part of this publication may be reproduced in whole or in part without express written consent of the publisher.

All scripture references are the King James Version unless otherwise noted.

Published by Metamorphosis Publishing & Consulting, LLC
P. O. Box 963
Redan, Georgia 30074

Book Cover created by Lloyd Owens
Edited by Kimberly Hughes, Judah's Writings Unlimited & Akeia Simmons

For ministry or books:

Ministry: Email – barrenbreaking@aol.com

Books: Email- metamorphpublishing@yahoo.com

DEDICATION

I would like to dedicate this book to:

My Lord and Saviour Jesus Christ, the BARREN BREAKER in my life and author and finisher of my faith…our love is eternal. Thank you for trusting me to carry your seed in the earth. I will never betray our covenant.

The love of my life, Derek Howard – one impartation of your love changed the course of my life forever.

&

The barren breaking girls who broke the womb: Keturah and Amariah….Oh how mommy loves you! You will forever break down the walls of "No".

The Birthing Process

CONTENTS

DEDICATION
CONTENTS
FOREWORD
    Pastor Derek Howard
    Apostle Bill Howard
    Apostle Judy Shaw
THE BIRTHING PROCESS DEFINED
INTRODUCTION

CHAPTERS   **Page**

THE FIRST TRIMESTER
CHAPTER 1: Nothing but the Blood of Jesus………………….18
CHAPTER 2: It's Time for the Hemorrhaging to Stop…………49
CHAPTER 3: Are you Willing to Carry the Baby Full Term…...80
CHAPTER 4: D.I.E. (Decrease in Everything)…………………92
CHAPTER 5: Barren on Purpose…………………………….....101
CHAPTER 6: The Birthing of Barren Breaking Ministries…….110

THE SECOND TRIMESTER
CHAPTER 7: FEAR: Spiritual Birth Control………………….124
CHAPTER 8: The Woman, the Seed and the Serpent…………137
CHAPTER 9: The Day of Conception…………………………162
CHAPTER 10: Until you Perceive you Can't Conceive……….173
CHAPTER 11: This Looks like a Job for El Shaddai………….181
CHAPTER 12: Whose Seed is in Itself………………………...212

CHAPTER 13: Spiritual Miscarriage- What Happened
                to the Seed?..237

THE THIRD TRIMESTER
CHAPTER 14: Braxton-Hicks – False Contractions...........…...249
CHAPTER 15: The Labor Pains and the Gift......................260
CHAPTER 16: Stage 1 – Early Labor, Active Labor and
                   Transitioning..279
CHAPTER 17: Stage 2- Pushing......................................289
CHAPTER 18: Stage 3- Delivering of the Placenta.............298
CHAPTER 19: Giving Birth to a Breech Nation................308
CHAPTER 20: More About the Afterbirth......................327

REFERENCES...337

ACKNOWLEDGEMENTS..…......339

FOREWORD

This book is a must-read for both believers and non-believers that seek a closer relationship with Christ and clarity regarding the process of spiritual birthing. Tapika does a masterful job of walking the reader through the stages of the birthing process by simultaneously building our faith and understanding through the Word of God and practical experience.

My excitement about this book is twofold. First, as a Christian, I realize that an understanding and successful application of the spiritual birthing process is integral to the growth and development of believers everywhere. I know that this book will enable those that read it to acquire the tools necessary to reach their maximum potential in God. Secondly, as Tapika's husband of 17 years, I have had an up close and personal view of this process operating in our lives collectively and individually. I have witnessed in her the type of maturation that only comes from a consistent, committed walk with God. Time and time again I have seen her employ the very principles which she imparts to the reader through this book in order to produce fruit in her own life.

So enjoy and let the birthing begin!

Pastor Derek Howard
Integrity Christian Ministries
Jonesboro, Georgia

FOREWORD

I've known and watched Prophetess Tapika Howard since the inception of this divine conception. Since the times of infancy in operating in the prophetic gifts; she has been a yielded vessel to disseminate the Gospel of our Lord Jesus Christ.

I've likened the prophetic gift God has given her as one that has budded; bloomed and blossomed.

As nine is the prophetic number that represents the fruit of things and is noted for divine completeness. I look forward to her next book with great anticipation to see and enjoy the fruit of her labor that has come full circle to divine fruition.

Apostle Bill Howard
Church of the Living Way
Union City, Georgia

FOREWORD

Genesis 30:1, Gives a desperate, determined cry from the heart of a woman. With a loud passionate voice, not fully understanding the magnitude of this hearts cry, Rachael yells out *"...Give me Child, or else I die!"* She's addressing her husband Jacob, the one and only person who can end her agony of barrenness. Before we tell you about the baby which Rachael conceived and bore, let's follow Tapika into the delivery room! WE ARE NOW IN THE BIRTHING PROCESS!

The Birthing Process is a book that accurately shows and points us to the "Now" season that we presently are in. Many have called this season, Harvest time, Reaping time, Due Season, and even End time Fulfillment. Tapika reveals and unfolds to us the urgency of knowing what to do during this very crucial season. It's the age old question of "How" that we all tend to wonder or ask about as we attempt to safely journey to our destiny.

Tapika Howard, having both natural and spiritual children, has uttered the same words as Rachael. Tapika, knowing that she was born to produce, born to birth and to leave something significant and eternal into this world, once again, she begins to put ink to her personal experience, thoughts and God given revelation. As she births this book into the world, through love and labor, with passion and precision, patience and urgency, she releases the instruments and tools needed for the BIRTHING

PROCESS.

From the beginning until the very end, this book introduces practical steps and insightful information to enable every reader to be prepared and ready for his or her delivery. My prayer is that you read this, do this, learn this and like my spiritual daughter Tapika, while in the birthing process, bare down, grunt, scream and say within yourself......I was born to produce, and I will have my Destiny!

Now...let the Birthing Process Begin!

Apostle Judy Shaw
Center of Life Church International
Sioux Falls, South Dakota

The Birthing Process Defined

The Birthing Process is the spiritual process that every believer must endure to see the full manifestation of the promise. The birthing process is gender-less. It applies to both male and female alike. It provides a detailed description of the process that is required to carry the promises of God, from the point of conception in prayer, until it is made flesh and dwells among the believer as a tangible reality.

In the natural, a pregnancy is broken into three periods, or trimesters, each of about three months. As it relates to the Spiritual Birthing Process, the Spirit of the Lord has broken it into three phases: **spiritual intercourse**, **conception** and **delivery**. Once the semen of the Word of God is released, a choice must be made; will you miscarry or carry that which has been planted full-term.

As you read this book, you will gain an understanding of God's divine will for every scripture, (which is spiritual semen), that is released in your spirit! God not only desires to impregnate you, but for you to carry His Word until the point of delivery. The Birthing Process Book will give you the divine instruction from the Holy Spirit on how to carry it out; and walk out of the delivery room holding the tangible evidence!

INTRODUCTION

INTRODUCTION

If this book has landed into your hands, I have been instructed to serve as what God considers your personal spiritual midwife. I am on an assignment by the Almighty God to provide you with detailed instructions regarding this baby (vision, dream, prophesy or promise from God) you are carrying and by the time you are finished with this book, then the process of how to deliver a baby will be made known to you.

I have been on a quest for over 15 years as a spiritual midwife to ensure the safe delivery of many "babies" from the spirit realm. These "babies" ranged from a woman's desire to obtain a real baby in the natural to someone who desires to give birth to a multi-million dollar business. All of which have occurred because of my obedience in intercession for others. However, I have also witnessed many spiritual abortions, miscarriages and even those who rejected the semen of His Word. These incidents occurred because although many have been given intercessors to assist them in this process, no one can carry, nurture and birth for you. You must be willing and obedient to eat the good of the land and birth out the promises of God yourself. Even for me, my assignment as a spiritual midwife came during a time in my life where barrenness was as far as I could see. However,

God's plan for my life would be to bring me to an expected end. This end would include me teaching others how to give birth through prayer and intercession. Honestly, I didn't see this one coming. Each day was simply a walk of faith.

There are **two things** you can be assured of after reading this book: Your expectation shall not be denied and you will give birth! **Some of you may have to walk it out by faith before you see it.** Despite what method has to be used to get the promise out, NOW IS THE APPOINTED TIME!

The scripture says in Isaiah 66:7-9 (NKJV), *"Before she was in labor, she gave birth; Before her pain came, She delivered a male child. Who has heard such a thing? Who has seen such things? Shall the earth be made to give birth in one day? Or shall a nation be born at once? For as soon as Zion was in labor, She gave birth to her children. Shall I bring to the time of birth, and not cause delivery?" says the LORD. Shall I who cause delivery shut up the womb?" says your God."* As a member of the commonwealth society of the kingdom of God, and one who has been created in His image, **you were birthed to give birth. You were born to produce.** Your assignment in the earth has always been **to produce after His kind. It is the LAW** (Genesis 1:26-28). To produce after any other kind except **His kind,** is against the LAW. You can no longer break the LAW! The earth is waiting, people are waiting and the DELIVERER in you is waiting for the LAW to be established in your heart and mind. I decree and declare to you today, that this book will provoke you to give birth in **one day**, what you have tried to birth for years.

Many of you have experienced **intense labor pains** over the past few months and some even years. However, **pain is the Believer's midwife** and must be in place to make room for the release that is in the birth canal of the Father. Jesus Christ Himself was in the birth canal of the Father. He had to endure in agony and pain the Garden of Gethsemane and Calvary **before** His resurrection. Christ in you is the hope of glory. You too, like Jesus and like a woman in labor, must endure with patience and perseverance to obtain the promise. There is one thing for sure: **Once the baby is in the birth canal – there is no turning back.** I know your promise has reached the birth canal because the pain has almost been unbearable.

The pain for the Believer comes before the breaking through of the waters. Your pain has opened the door for the waters to break through. I BELIEVE YOUR WATER HAS BROKEN and out of your belly shall flow the eternal river of living waters. These living waters shall cause you to birth this new thing in God and even resurrect dead things. As a matter of fact, the Holy Spirit shall perform a spiritual C-section on many of you while you are reading. Why? This delivery shall not be like those in the past. **It weighs more, it costs more and it belongs to God. It has His DNA.** This next move and delivery from God shall not be by might, nor by power, but by His Spirit! No man will get the glory out of this one....GOD WANTS THE GLORY and has allowed circumstances to come to ensure it.

    I believe by the Spirit that this book will serve as a delivery room for many. **In the delivery room, the manifestation of the promise is ASSURED!** So hold on tight, put your feet in the spiritual stirrups and bear down.....it's time to PUSH OUT and DELIVER every promise from God! The Parakletos (Holy Spirit) is here to help and Jesus Christ alone will BE GLORIFIED! Come take a journey with me as I reveal the steps you must take in *"The Birthing Process"* to ensure the safe arrival of what God promised. In Jesus Name,

Prophetess Tapika M. Howard
Barren Breaking Ministries, Inc.
Founder & Spiritual Midwife

THE FIRST TRIMESTER

Natural Law: In medicine, the First Trimester is defined as the beginning when the developing embryo becomes implanted into the endometrial lining of a woman's uterus. This is the most susceptible time for a woman to miscarry during the $1^{st} - 3^{rd}$ months.

Spiritual Law: It is simply when the impregnable Truth is received in the Spirit (womb) of an individual. Thereby, leaving evidence of the penetration; a sure seed (Romans 4:16). However, because this is a very sensitive phase, the ability to nurture the seed with the Word of God will determine whether the seed will grow and remain.

Chapter 1: The Prerequisite:
"Nothing but the Blood of Jesus"

"Nothing but the Blood of Jesus"

There are lyrics to an old hymn that still ring in my ears from the time I was a little girl going to the neighborhood Baptist church with my grandmother. Unfortunately, due to lack of understanding, it was just another church song to me then and did not mean much. Although I noticed the longer the choir sang the lyrics in complete harmony and unison, the more people would weep uncontrollably and lose their ability to stand erect. The hymn still did not move me like that, but I expected that I did not know the impact the song had on the lives of those within the church pews. However, during the time we were trying to become pregnant, those lyrics became real and when heard or thought of today remind me of the foundation of my eternal redemption. As well as the privilege it afforded me to endure the birthing process for my life and give birth to every promise from God. As a matter of fact, Christians would not be a part of the kingdom of God without the emphasis of the life-line provided in this song. The song says, *"What can wash away my sin? Nothing but the blood of Jesus; What can make me whole again? Nothing but the blood of Jesus. Oh! precious is the flow that makes me white as snow; No other fount I know, Nothing but the blood of Jesus."* Jesus was placed in the womb of Mary and for nine months took on flesh, appendages, a body, and organs. It amazes me that the woman's womb gave Him everything but blood. Anyone in medicine will tell you that the bloodline of a child is established through the father. Medically speaking, since this is true, the blood that Jesus had could not come from Joseph, because Joseph was not his father. The blood that Jesus carried could not come through Mary because it comes through the father's bloodline. So the blood that this glorious and wonderful seed carried had to be of a divine origin. Jesus didn't have O positive or AB positive. The blood of Jesus couldn't ever be grafted or analyzed by man. Jesus had a supernatural, divine bloodline that didn't come from a blood transfusion. His blood was pure, uncontaminated and undefiled because it came from the purest source, our Father, which is in heaven. For this reason, He knew no sin because sin was never a part of His bloodline. Because of this, His blood redeemed us from sin. We are the redeemed of the Lord; able to say what the Word says is so because of the blood of Jesus.

There is nothing but the blood of Jesus that can wash away sins. The blood of Jesus is the foundation of redemption. Jesus Christ died on the cross shedding His blood and was resurrected so that you and I could have access to life and that more abundantly. There is no other religion that has been or will ever be afforded this level of sacrifice. **The blood of Jesus was the <u>only</u>**

acceptable payment for the sins of the world. The blood of Jesus is the only way to salvation. No man can come to the Father, but by the name of Jesus. The scripture says in I Peter 1:18-19 in the New Living Translation, *"For you know that God paid a ransom to save you from the empty life you inherited from your ancestors. And the ransom he paid was not mere gold or silver. It was the precious blood of Christ, the sinless, spotless Lamb of God. God chose him as your ransom long before the world began, but he has now revealed him to you in these last days."* Christ became sin for us, while we were yet sinners. The scripture says in Romans 5:7-9, *"For scarcely for a righteous man will one die: yet peradventure for a good man some would even dare to die. But God commendeth his love toward us, in that, while we were yet sinners, Christ died for us. Much more then, being now justified by his blood, we shall be saved from wrath through him."* The payment that Christ made for our sins is irreparable. Yet, it is the least discussed in the church today. It is time for the Body of Christ to be reminded of why we are overcomers and more than conquerors today. It is simply because of the precious blood of the Lamb.

There is one assured thing about Christianity which gives it meaning and that is the blood of Jesus. The blood of Jesus is the spiritual semen for a Christians "blessed assurance." By no other way could the church have been conceived. The blood of Jesus is the only thing that gives life to the teaching and the power of the Word of God. It is because it is the power of God unto salvation and without acknowledgement of it, no man can be saved. However, there is one truth that must be made plain. The scripture says in Hebrews 4:12, *"For the word of God is quick, and powerful, and sharper than any two-edged sword, piercing even to the dividing asunder of soul and spirit, and of the joints and marrow, and is a discerner of the thoughts and intents of the heart."* The Word of God is quick. The word "quick" translated in this verse of scripture means "living or alive". The Word of God is a living word. This alone makes the bible unique and different. It is distinct because unlike any other book it contains blood circulating through every page, every chapter and every verse. This circulation of the blood begins in the book of Genesis and ends in the book of Revelation. Even to take it a step further, from the beginning to the end of the bible you see the stream of His blood which is an impartation of the very life of God. I began thinking that without the blood of Jesus, the bible would be like any other book with no value. However, the scripture says in Leviticus 17:11, *"For the life of the flesh is in the blood: and I have given it to you upon the altar to make an atonement for your souls for it is the blood that maketh an atonement for the soul."*

The blood of Jesus is what makes the bible priceless and the partakers that receive its eternal inscription.

The scripture says in Revelation 12:11, *"And they overcame him by the blood of the Lamb, and by the word of their testimony; and they loved not their lives unto the death."* The only way a person can live an overcoming life is through and by the blood of Jesus. The blood of Jesus has the power to save, protect, redeem and continuously cleanse (Revelation 7:14). It is the most precious gift God has offered to us. Despite the false numbers received from other religions of believers that will be saved and allowed entrance into heaven, you must know that it is possible for everyone to have the protection, healing, restoration and forgiveness that the blood of Jesus provides. **Despite even the sins and offenses that many have committed against God, <u>He offers</u> this gift to each of us.** The scripture says in John 3:16-17, *"For God so loved the world, that he gave his only begotten Son, that whosoever believeth in him should not perish, but have everlasting life. For God sent not his Son into the world to condemn the world; but that the world through him might be saved."* Every human born has sinned against God and fallen short of His glory. Yet, God provided an escape plan through Jesus Christ. The scripture says in Romans 3:20-26, *"Therefore by the deeds of the law there shall no flesh be justified in his sight: for by* *the law is the knowledge of sin. But now the righteousness of God without the law is manifested, being witnessed by the law and the prophets; Even the righteousness of God which is by faith of Jesus Christ unto all and upon all them that believe: for there is no difference: For all have sinned, and come short of the glory of God; Being justified freely by his grace through the redemption that is in Christ Jesus: Whom God hath set forth to be a propitiation through faith in his blood, to declare his righteousness for the remission of sins that are past, through the forbearance of God; To declare, I say, at this time his righteousness: that he might be just, and the justifier of him which believeth in Jesus."* The sins of the world did not stop Jesus, the sins of the world propelled Jesus in love to act. Therefore, He willed Himself to pay a debt He did not owe, because we owed a debt we could not pay. Now that is the glory of the Lord revealed in the earth to an undeserving people. This is a people who would under normal circumstances be pronounced guilty of all charges. Yet, the blood of Jesus provided a not guilty plea and eradicated every sin for which you and I should have been indicted. Thank you Jesus for your blood!

In one of my favorite books by Dr. M. R. DeHaan, entitled, "<u>The Chemistry of the Blood</u>", Dr. DeHaan describes the physiological state of the human blood like this, *"In the human body there are many different kinds of tissues. We define them as muscles, nerve, fat, gland, bone, connective tissues, etc. All these tissues have one thing in common; they are fixed cells, microscopically small and having a specific and limited function. Unlike these fixed tissues, the blood is fluid and mobile, that is, it is not limited to one part of the body but is free to move throughout the entire body and touch every other fixed cell as it supplies it with nourishment and carries off waste products and the ashes of cell activity which we call metabolism. In the normal human body there are about five pints of this fluid, and this blood pumped by the heart circulates through the system about every twenty-three seconds, so that every cell in the body is constantly supplied and cleansed and at the same time is in constant communication and touch with every other cell in that body. This blood is the most mysterious of all tissues, being composed of scores of elements and compounds and strange chemical bodies, whose function is not yet fully understood, but all of which have to do with the mystery of life for the "life is in the blood." Once the blood fails to reach the cells and members of the body, they promptly die and no man ever dies until his blood ceases to circulate. The life is in the blood."*

Dr. DeHaan's description of the human blood is succinctly connected to the blood of Jesus Christ that despite race, creed or national origin has the ability to operate as the cohesive life-line for every believer.

The scripture says in Acts 17:24-28, *"God that made the world and all things therein, seeing that he is Lord of heaven and earth, dwelleth not in temples made with hands; Neither is worshipped with men's hands, as though he needed anything, seeing he giveth to all life, and breath, and all things;* ***And hath made of one blood all nations of men for to dwell on all the face of the earth, and hath determined the times before appointed, and the bounds of their habitation;*** *That they should seek the Lord, if haply they might feel after him, and find him, though he be not far from every one of us: For in him we live, and move, and have our being; as certain also of your own poets have said, For we are also his offspring."* The blood of Jesus is the eternal transportation system that runs through every Christian which makes us a body that is fitly joined together. This is why the scripture tells us that there should be no schism or division in the body.

The scripture says in I Corinthians 12:24-26, *"For our comely parts have no need:* ***but God hath tempered the body together,*** *having given more abundant honour to that part which lacked.* ***That there should be no schism in the body; but that the members should have the same care one for another. And whether one member suffer, all the members suffer with it; or*** *one member be honoured, all the members rejoice with it."* You cannot separate the head from the body. Neither can you separate the blood from the body. In essence, in an attempt to separate the blood of Jesus from the Body of Christ, you cut off the eternal circulation and the "body" becomes non-existent! We must be cautious of this truth because the lack of discussion of the blood of Jesus almost implies its non-existence. LET ME MAKE A REDEMPTIVE ANNOUNCEMENT: **You cannot exist, you cannot live, and you cannot have the being of Christ in you, the hope of glory, without His blood!**

You cannot discuss the blood of Jesus without discussing why the blood was necessary in the first place. In the book of Genesis, you find the creation of man and the formation of woman from man. Both of whom were created in the image of God (Genesis 1:26-27). The scripture provides an excellent picturesque description of the moment when God created man in His image. The scripture says in Genesis 2:6-7, *"But there went up a mist from the earth, and watered the whole face of the ground. And the Lord formed man of the dust of the ground, and breathed into his nostrils the breath of life; and man became a living soul."* The scripture says that a mist came up and watered the whole face of the ground. Thereafter, the Lord formed man from the dust of the ground. This makes a strong implication to me that surely Adam was nothing less than a lump of mud or clay with no life and no ability to move. When water and dirt or dust is mixed together it becomes a substance that we all know as mud or clay. I am further moved to believe after reading the scriptures that Adam was simply a lump of clay with no life until God breathed into him. The potter had to do something else with the clay to bring it to life, so He breathed into the lifeless object and man became a living soul.

I mentioned earlier that **the life of the flesh is in the blood**. I believe by the Spirit that when God breathed into Adam, He put something in him to make him come alive. I am compelled to believe that something was the blood. The blood is what gave Adam life. Most theologians say it was the breath of God that brought life. However, in studying the breathing mechanism of the human body, I discovered that there are two processes at work as we breathe in and breathe out. **Blood vessels transport blood that is rich in carbon dioxide** and poor in oxygen to the alveoli. In the reverse process, the carbon dioxide goes out through the walls of the alveoli, into the airways, and, as we breathe out, back up the trachea. Furthermore, the heart then pumps the oxygen-rich blood through the body and we are able to do things like run up a hill, throw a ball, or even exercise. Therefore, when God breathed into Adam, He provided the first blood transfusion and again man became a living soul.

Once Adam ate from the tree of knowledge and sinned, the blood that was flowing through him became contaminated. Prior to this, Adam's blood was pure and undefiled because God breathed into Adam, imparting into Adam all that He was – which was clean, undefiled and without sin. In reading another part of Dr. DeHaan's book, <u>The Chemistry of the Blood,</u> it became clear. Adam died spiritually when he fell short of the glory of God and when he did something happened to his blood. Although the body functions and operates effectively because of the blood, the sin directly affected the blood of man, not his body. This is why you read in Matthew, Chapter 23, the account of Jesus' rebuke of the Pharisees. The scripture says in Matthew 23:25, *"Woe unto you, scribes and Pharisees, hypocrites! for ye make clean the outside of the cup and of the platter, but within they are full of extortion and excess. Thou blind Pharisee, cleanse first that which is within the cup and platter, that the outside of them may be clean also."* Jesus was telling them that it is not what is on the outside of a man that makes him unclean, but it is what comes from within a man that makes him unclean and can destroy him. For example, if you never say how you really feel about someone you dislike and you are pretending all is well, it is not what they see on the outside that will harm them or you. It is what is on the inside of you that will contaminate your heart and still leave them unaffected.

Due to the fall of the first Adam, God's plan to redeem man back unto Himself required the help of a woman. It is amazing to me that it was the woman who was enticed by the flattering words of the serpent and yielded to his enticement by eating of the tree of good and evil, thereby aborting the initial plan of God. Yet, God's plan would require a virgin woman to transport the answer to redemption. In so doing, the virgin woman, Mary, would once again, like Eve, have a verbal encounter. However, this time, the verbal encounter would be with the angel Gabriel, who was sent to announce the plan of redemption, which she would conceive by the Spirit, carry and birth out. I further realized why a virgin was required to conceive the redemptive plan. I mentioned earlier that when Adam fell sin was in his blood. He was impregnated with sin. Jesus could not be part of that lineage. The scripture says in Hebrews 4:15, *"For we have not an high priest which cannot be touched with the feeling of our infirmities; but was in all points tempted lie as we are,* **yet without sin.***"* If Jesus was without sin, God had to find another way to get Him in the earth without sin. The scripture says in Psalm 51:5, *"Behold, I was shapen in iniquity; and in sin did my mother conceive me."* Why did this verse of scripture not apply to the birth of Jesus Christ? The scripture says in Galatians 4:4-7, *"But when the fullness of the time* *was come, God sent forth his Son, made of a woman, made under the law, To redeem them that were under the law, that we might receive the adoption of sons. And because ye are sons, God hath sent forth the Spirit of his Son into you hearts, crying, Abba, Father. Wherefore thou art no more a servant, but a son; and if a son, then an heir of God through Christ."* So God found a way for Jesus to be born of a woman. The virgin birth was simply so that Christ would not have to partake of Adam's blood which was impregnated with sin. If sin was to be atoned for, it had to come through sinless blood. It had to come through one who was totally unaffected by Adam's sin and yet belong to the human race. This fully explains why Jesus is touched by the feelings of our infirmities because He had to walk the earth as a member of the human race, yet shed His blood to be resurrected as King. Now I further understand why we have to repent in Jesus name when we sin. It is so that the pure blood that was shed for our redemption can redeem us to our rightful position of righteousness when we fall short of his plan, purpose and His Word. By this, you should know that the love of God for you is persistent.

    I discovered another very interesting revelation as I studied God's formation of woman from man in the book of Genesis. In the book of Genesis 2:21-22, in the Amplified Bible, the scripture says, *"And the Lord God caused a deep sleep to fall upon Adam;*

and while he slept, He took one of his ribs or a part of his side and closed up the [place with] flesh. And the rib or part of his side which the Lord God had taken from the man He built up and made into a woman, and He brought her to the man." In these verses of scripture we discover that the Lord caused a deep sleep to fall upon Adam and while he slept God took a rib from a part of his side and used it to create woman. It is very important that I stop here and provide some natural dynamics regarding the ribs in the human body. The ribs in the human body are comprised of 24 bones arranged in 12 pairs. The number 12 represents governmental perfection, authority and rulership.

In studying the human anatomy, I found that these bones are uniquely divided into three categories. The first seven bones are called the *true ribs*. They are connected to the spine (the backbone) in the back. In the front, the *true ribs* are connected directly to the breastbone or sternum by strips of cartilage called the costal cartilage. The next three pairs of bones are called *false ribs*. These bones are slightly shorter than the true ribs and are connected to the spine in back. However, instead of being attached directly to the sternum in front, the false ribs are attached to the lowest true rib. The last two sets of rib bones are called *floating ribs*. I discovered that *floating ribs* are smaller than both the true ribs and the false ribs. They are attached to the spine at the back, but are not connected to anything in the front. Furthermore, the ribs help you to breathe. As you inhale, the muscles in between the ribs lift the rib cage up, allowing the lungs to expand. When you exhale, the rib cage moves down again, squeezing the air out of your lungs. In essence, God's plan to extract woman from the side or rib of man was to impart governmental perfection, authority and rulership into the earth. However, when they sinned the body was stripped of this dominant impartation. I will provide further understanding regarding this later.

In the book of John, Chapter 19, during the crucifixion of Christ, you find something being released from Jesus' side too, which is not coincidental. The scripture says in John 19:33-34, *"But when they came to Jesus, and saw that he was dead already, they brake not his legs: But one of the soldiers with a spear pierced his side, and forthwith came there out blood and water."* When the soldier pierced Jesus in his side, out of His side came blood and water. The first Adam had his side opened while he was in a deep sleep and God used his ribs to create a bride that was taken out. The last Adam, Jesus Christ, was pierced in His side while He was in a deep sleep of death and God used His blood to create a bride, (the church) that was taken out. This bride is known as the "Body of Christ".

The scripture says in Revelation 21:9, *"And there came*

unto me one of the seven angels which had the seven vials full of the seven last plagues, and talked with me, saying, **Come hither, I will shew thee the bride, the Lamb's wife.**" In God's redemptive plan to **show the bride** in the manner He ordained from the beginning, He did not forget to buy back the governmental perfection, authority, and rulership and place it where it belongs. The scripture further states in Revelation 1:4-6, *"John to the seven churches which are in Asia: Grace be unto you, and peace, from him which is, and which was, and which is to come; and from the seven Spirits which are before his throne; And from Jesus Christ, who is the faithful witness, and the first begotten of the dead, and the prince of the kings of the earth. Unto him that loved us, and washed us from our sins in his own blood, And hath made us kings and priests unto God and His Father; to him be glory and dominion for ever and ever. Amen."* Then in Revelation 21:10-14, we see the realignment of order and God's governmental authority in the earth. The scripture says, *"And he carried me away in the spirit to a great and high mountain, and shewed me that great city, the holy Jerusalem, descending out of heaven from God, Having the glory of God: and her light was like unto a stone most precious, even like a jasper stone, clear as crystal; And had a wall great and high, and* **had twelve gates**, **and at the gates twelve angels,** *and names written thereon, which are the names of the* twelve tribes of the children of Israel: **On the east three gates; on the north three gates; on the south three gates; and on the west three gates. And the wall of the city had twelve foundations, and in them the names of the twelve apostles of the Lamb.*"* It is no accident or coincidence that at every entrance God made it known that He has given the authority to us and we are kings and priests unto our God. Yet, the foundation of which is discussed in Revelation, Chapter 21, is the same foundation that is discussed in the book of Ephesians, Chapter 2.

The scripture says in Ephesians 2:13-22, *"But now in Christ Jesus ye who sometimes were far off are made nigh by the blood of Christ. For he is our peace, who hath made both one, and hath broken down the middle wall of partition between us; Having abolished in his flesh the enmity, even the law of commandments contained in ordinances; for to make in himself of twain one new man, so making peace; And that he might reconcile both unto God in one body by the cross, having slain the enmity thereby: And came and preached peace to you which were afar off, and to them that were nigh. For through him we both have access by one Spirit unto the Father. Now therefore ye are no more strangers and foreigners, but fellowcitizens with the saints, and of the household of God;* **And are built upon the foundation of the apostles and prophets, Jesus Christ himself being the chief corner stone;** *In* *whom all the building fitly framed together groweth unto an holy temple in the Lord: In whom ye also are builded together for an habitation of God through the Spirit."* Out of Christ came blood and water so that the foundation of the church could be re-established, re-deemed, and re-vived!

Once I assessed the bible from Genesis to Revelation, I discovered that even when it was not mentioned, the blood of Jesus ran like a scarlet thread through the entire book. It was moving through every chapter, verse and scripture even when it was not mentioned. In the book of Genesis, Chapter 4, you find the sacrifices that Cain and Abel brought. Although Abel's sacrifice was accepted, Cain's was rejected because there was no blood involved (Genesis 4:1-10). This explains why the blood of Abel was crying from the ground because God accepted his sacrifice as holy, pure and undefiled. Yet, Cain's sacrifice was not and sin was at the door and entrance of his heart. Then in Genesis, Chapter 9, Noah does something that grabs God's attention. He sheds the blood of the clean animals out of the Ark and God so faithfully makes a covenant of grace with him (Genesis 9:1-17). In the book of Genesis, Chapter 22, Abraham discovers a ram in the bushes that he uses for Isaac's substitute and the blood of the ram or the blood of the substitute spares the sinner (Genesis 22:4-13).

In the book of Exodus we find the Passover Lamb. God

instructed Israel to slay lambs on the night of the Passover in Egypt (Exodus 12:6 and Numbers 12:6). He then instructed them to take the blood of the lambs and place it upon the doorpost and lentil to cover the houses and secure the entire household as God executed judgment on the first-born of every man and beast in Egypt (Exodus 12:7, 22-23; Exodus 12:12-13). The lamb was termed in that time as the "Passover Sacrifice" (Exodus 12:21, 27). In obedience to the Lord, each home covered with the blood of the slain lamb, was protected, spared and passed over as the Lord passed through the land with judgment. I must interject right here. Think it not strange that you have been protected from the visible and the invisible forces that were sent to cancel the plan of God for your life. Think it not strange that you have been protected from foreclosure, social economic collapse and financial ruins. It is simply because of the blood of Jesus that you have been spared, protected and passed over! This alone warrants an exceptional praise to the Most High God!

Let me finish showing you how the blood of Jesus has run like a scarlet thread throughout the bible. In the book of Exodus and Leviticus you find the tabernacle sacrifices with streams of blood. As a matter of fact, the scripture says in Exodus 29:38-42, *"Now this is that which thou shalt offer upon the altar; two lambs of the first year day by day continually. The one lamb thou shalt offer in the morning; and the other lamb thou shalt offer at even: And with the one lamb a tenth deal of flour mingled with the fourth part of an hin of beaten oil; and the fourth part of an hin of wine for a drink offering. And the other lamb thou shalt offer at even, and shalt do thereto according to the meat offering of the morning, and according to the drink offering thereof, for a sweet savour, an offering made by fire unto the LORD. This shall be a continual burnt offering throughout your generations at the door of the tabernacle of the congregation before the LORD: where I will meet you, to speak there unto thee."* You will find many scriptures throughout the bible where the lamb or his blood was offered as a sacrifice. All throughout the bible you trace the blood steps of the lamb until you see on Calvary God's perfect lamb of which all the others were a prototype or a picture. The Lamb of God who was slain for the sins of the world was God's own gift, who died in the place of others and shed His own precious blood. It was the release of a three-fold cord that would not be broken.

The scripture says in Luke 22:44, *"And being in agony he prayed more earnestly: and his sweat was as it were great drops of blood falling down to the ground."* First, I realized why Luke provided this bloody description of Jesus' sweat. If you have studied anything about the natural professions of the disciples, you would be reminded that Luke was a physician. So his description of Jesus' agony in the Garden of Gethsemane was not figurative but literally medical. How am I so sure about this? For those of you who are avid readers of what God releases through me from week to week, you know that I am a researcher by nature.

In doing research on the sweat glands, I found a rather interesting truth. Dr. Frederick Zugibe, Chief Medical Examiner of Rockland County, New York wrote this: "Although this medical condition is relatively rare, it is well-known, and there have been many cases of it. The clinical term is *"hematohidrosis."* Around the sweat glands, there are multiple blood vessels in a net-like form." Under the pressure of great stress the vessels constrict. Then as the anxiety passes, "the blood vessels dilate to the point of rupture. The blood goes into the sweat glands." As the sweat glands are producing a lot of sweat, it pushes the blood to the surface - coming out as droplets of blood mixed with sweat." Many deny that Jesus could have every sweat blood. However, this medical information proves otherwise.

Why is this so important to the believer today? Those great drops of blood that came from Jesus sweat were instrumental in your deliverance and mine today. As a matter of fact, those great drops of blood were instrumental in setting us as a people free from rebellion, fear and stubbornness, in our moments of weakness. It is when we are weak before God that He manifests

Himself as the God of strength (II Corinthians 12:8-10). Man became weak in the garden and fell short of the glory of God. Therefore, God had to manifest Himself as the God of strength by sending His only begotten Son to redeem man back to Himself. What a mighty God we serve!

In the book of John 19:30, the scripture says, *"When Jesus therefore had received the vinegar, he said, It is finished: and he bowed his head, and gave up the ghost."* There are a couple of things I want to address here. When Jesus said, *"It is finished"*, I honestly believe He was speaking in terms of His blood that had finished the work that was started in the garden in the book of Genesis. I am convinced that Philippians 1:6 applied to this very moment. The scripture says, *"Being confident of this very thing, that he which hath begun a good work in you will perform it until the day of Jesus Christ."* Furthermore, when Jesus gave up the ghost, it was as if He took His last breath and released something. Just like God breathed into Adam the breath of life, it was the blood of Jesus that was once again released into the earth, undefiled and untainted, as He departed the earth carrying the sins of the world. This time it was the manifested presence of the Holy Spirit that He left so that He could be resurrected on the third day. Yet, because the life of the flesh is in the blood, Jesus had to breathe out a manifestation of Himself so that when He was resurrected He would not receive contaminated blood, but a pure and undefiled impartation.

This explains the scripture in Hebrews 6:13 that says, *"For when God made promise to Abraham, **because he could swear by no greater, he sware by himself.**"* He swore by Himself because there was no greater sacrifice than His own blood. Now I am assured in my Spirit that this is why He gave up the ghost because it was a type of releasing of Himself into the earth. This is the same thing God did in the beginning. He released His image into the creation of man so that He could live, move and be like a "god" in the earth. Oh my God! How am I so sure? The scripture says in II Corinthians 3:17-18, *"Now the Lord is that Spirit: and where the Spirit of the Lord is, there is liberty. But we all, with open face beholding as in a glass the glory of the Lord, are changed into the same image from glory to glory, even as by the Spirit of the Lord."* Where ever the blood of Jesus is, there is freedom and there is liberty. For whom the Son has set free is free indeed. Where ever the Spirit of the Lord is there is liberty.

Although the Holy Spirit does not need blood to flow through Him to operate, He does need the traits of what Christ represents to resurrect the dead and to manifest liberty. If for no other reason other than they are one. The scripture tells us in I John 5:6-8, *"This is he that came by water and blood, even Jesus*

Christ; not by water only, but by water and blood. And it is the Spirit that beareth witness, because the Spirit is truth. For there are three that bear record in heaven, the Father, the Word, and the Holy Ghost: and these three are one. And there are three that bear witness in the earth, the spirit, and the water, and the blood: and these three agree in one." It is the Spirit of the Lord that bears witness with Jesus Christ, who came not by water only, but by water and blood. There are three that bear record and keeps record in heaven and it is the Father, the Son (the Word) and the Holy Ghost. Remember, the scripture says in John 14:9, *"....he that hath seen me hath seen the Father; and how sayest thou then, Shew us the Father?"* If you have seen Christ, you have seen the Father. If you have seen Christ, you have seen the Holy Spirit. They are one. They are inseparable. Then, there are three that bear witness in the earth and that is the spirit, water and the blood who are in total agreement as one entity. As it is in heaven, so shall it be in the earth. Jesus Christ and the Holy Spirit are in agreement. Therefore, when Jesus took His last breath, He released the blood and a manifestation of Himself, which was the Holy Spirit, to resurrect Him, just like He would resurrect the church with His blood. Our God is truly amazing and His plan is strategic and without fail.

Let me give you what you need to walk in a new level of

authority. The nails that were placed in the hands and feet of Jesus represent authority. The nails were used as an unchangeable instrument by the enemy to bind Jesus to the cross. Yet, because Jesus willed Himself to go through the Calvary encounter, the nails gave us all power over the enemy (Luke 10:19, Colossians 2:14-15).

The scripture says in John 20:19-29, *"Then the same day at evening, being the first day of the week,* **when the doors were shut** *where the disciples were assembled for fear of the Jews,* **came Jesus and stood in the midst, and saith unto them, Peace be unto you.** *And when he had so said, he shewed unto them his hands and his side. Then were the disciples glad, when they saw the LORD. Then said Jesus to them again, Peace be unto you: as my Father hath sent me, even so send I you.* **And when he had said this, he breathed on them, and saith unto them, Receive ye the Holy Ghost:** *Whose soever sins ye remit, they are remitted unto them; and whose soever sins ye retain, they are retained. But Thomas, one of the twelve, called Didymus, was not with them when Jesus came. The other disciples therefore said unto him, We have seen the LORD. But he said unto them, Except I shall see in his hands the print of the nails, and put my finger into the print of the nails, and thrust my hand into his side, I will not believe. And after eight days again his disciples were within, and Thomas with them:* **then**

came Jesus, the doors being shut, and stood in the midst, and said, Peace be unto you. *Then saith he to Thomas, Reach hither thy finger, and behold my hands; and reach hither thy hand, and thrust it into my side: and be not faithless, but believing. And Thomas answered and said unto him, My LORD and my God. Jesus saith unto him, Thomas, because thou hast seen me, thou hast believed: blessed are they that have not seen, and yet have believed."* I just want you to visualize this one thing. Yes, we know that Jesus had not ascended to the Father, so He was not in the natural form that the disciples had last seen Him.

These scriptures make a powerful statement. As you yield and allow every member to be put to death you are able to walk in the authority afforded to you by Christ. When you die in the flesh for the glory of God, you are still alive in your Spirit. Therefore, you have the ability to go through doors that no man can shut (Revelation 3:7). What point am I making? The blood of Jesus provides access to the impossible and brings clarity to who you really are in Him. The scripture says in Mark 15:37-39, *"And Jesus cried with a loud voice, and gave up the ghost. And the veil of the temple was rent in twain from the top to the bottom. And when the centurion, which stood over against him, saw that he so cried out, and gave up the ghost, he said, Truly this man was the Son of God."* When the veil of the temple was torn from the top to the bottom, you and I were given access. This means without a mediator or a priest, we could now go beyond the veil and into the holy of holies because of the blood of Jesus.

In Dr. Bree Keyton's book entitled, <u>Stripes, Nails, Thorns and the Blood</u>, she provides an eternal description of the crown of thorns that I have studied for years and each year the Spirit of the Lord provides yet another revelation. The crown of thorns placed on the head of Christ during the crucifixion was an all-out attack on the soulish realm. This includes your mind, will, emotions, imagination and memory. If you have never read the message the Lord gave me entitled, *"Make Up Your Mind"*, it openly addresses God's intense revelation about the natural and renewed mind. It is in the soulish realm where the real battle normally takes place. The thorns represent the hindrances, evil circumstances and cares of this life.

The scripture says in John 19:2-3, *"And the soldiers platted a crown of thorns, and put it on his head, and they put on him a purple robe. And said, Hail, King of the Jews! and they smote him with their hands."* I now understand why the scripture tells us that He had no place to lay His head because of the excruciating pain He must have felt as the thorns pierced His flesh. Christ did all of this for you and I. The thorns and the thistles were part of the curse and a sign of sin. In Genesis, Chapter 3, you find God cursing the serpent, and judging Adam and Eve for the fall. Then the scripture says in Genesis 3:18, *"Thorns also and thistles shall it bring forth to thee; and thou shalt eat the herb of the field."* Yet, despite this fall, Jesus, who knew no sin became sin for us that we might have eternal life.

Jesus bore the curse on His head that we might possess the mind of Christ in I Corinthians 2:16. The blood from the wound that the thorns created fell on the ground to cleanse it and deliver us from the curse. In essence, the thorns became our helmet of salvation (Ephesians 6:17). This is why daily you have a right to let THIS mind be in you, which was also in Christ Jesus. This is why you have the power to cast down every imagination and high thing that exalts itself against the knowledge of God and bring every thought captive unto the obedience of Christ. The obedience of Christ was the shedding of His blood for your mental deliverance and mine.

As I continued to study and read all the scriptures regarding the blood of Jesus, I kept noticing that everywhere the redemptive blood touched, something was made free. Even the blood that was on the back of Jesus from the 39 stripes that were created from lashings He received from the Roman whip, bear deliverance for you and I.

The scripture says in Isaiah 53:1-10, *"Who hath believed*

our report? and to whom is the arm of the LORD revealed? For he shall grow up before him as a tender plant, and as a root out of a dry ground: he hath no form nor comeliness; and when we shall see him, there is no beauty that we should desire him. He is despised and rejected of men; a man of sorrows, and acquainted with grief: and we hid as it were our faces from him; he was despised, and we esteemed him not. Surely he hath borne our griefs, and carried our sorrows: yet we did esteem him stricken, smitten of God, and afflicted. But he was wounded for our transgressions, he was bruised for our iniquities: the chastisement of our peace was upon him; **and with his stripes we are healed.** All we like sheep have gone astray; we have turned every one to his own way; and the LORD hath laid on him the iniquity of us all. He was oppressed, and he was afflicted, yet he opened not his mouth: he is brought as a lamb to the slaughter, and as a sheep before her shearers is dumb, so he openeth not his mouth. He was taken from prison and from judgment: and who shall declare his generation? for he was cut off out of the land of the living: for the transgression of my people was he stricken. And he made his grave with the wicked, and with the rich in his death; because he had done no violence, neither was any deceit in his mouth. Yet it pleased the LORD to bruise him; he hath put him to grief: when thou shalt make his soul an offering for sin, he shall see his seed, *he shall prolong his days, and the pleasure of the LORD shall prosper in his hand."* The stripes of Jesus won back our health, liberty, peace, prosperity and all else. We were snatched out of the hands of humiliation, embarrassment and oppression because Jesus opened not His mouth but yielded so that in any situation you would have the victory and absolute freedom. I believe that everyone who reads this timely Word from the Lord will see freedom manifest in areas of your life that appear to be **barren**, dead, lifeless and without peace.

Today, God is breathing into your life with His Word and you shall live and not die and declare the works of the living God. You shall see, hear and experience the results of the power of His blood like never before in this season. Yet, you must acknowledge the blood of Jesus, even as you acknowledge your Christianity. There is no separation between the two. They are one.

Chapter 2: "It's Time for the Hemorrhaging to Stop"

"It's Time for the Hemorrhaging to Stop"

As many of you know, we have found ourselves in a very pivotal moment in the Body of Christ. This is the year that God has positioned us to recover all. In the book of I Samuel, Chapter 30, you find David, doing a work for the Lord. When he got back from battle, all of his goods were stolen. I know many of you who have been doing the will of God feel the same way...that while you have been doing a work for the Lord, it appears as if an enemy has come and stolen all of your goods. Well I have good news in that respect; this is that year that God has declared that if you pursue Him, without hesitation, obstruction or delay, YOU SHALL RECOVER ALL!

While all of that may be truth and we have been positioned for forward victories, there are some past defeats that keep getting in the way. My assignment in this chapter is to take you and your heart on a journey far away from yesterday into the land of fertility and fruitfulness, with no bleeding spiritually, emotionally, physically or relationally. God desires for us as members of the Body of Christ, to be whole in every aspect of our lives. However, I am finding as I travel and meet other believers that our spiritual lives and our natural lives are totally out of balanced. Last season was full of opposition, but it was really a time for a tune-up to get you into proper alignment for the victories that would be birthed ahead. So God is not just after ensuring that you be made whole, but that you live what you speak, you have what you speak and you hold what you desire. In order to do that the light of the Word of God must illuminate some truth and expose things that have for years been out of alignment and have caused hemorrhaging in areas where you have produced little, to no fruit.

In the book of Mark, Chapter 5, I discovered something that is vitally important to movement and I want to discuss in detail in this chapter of <u>The Birthing Process</u> book. I believe that the Spirit of the Lord will use this chapter of the book to navigate out of you the very thing that has hindered productivity and prohibited mobility in certain areas of your life.

The scripture says in Mark 5:25-34, *"And a certain woman, which had an issue of blood for twelve years. And had suffered many things of many physicians, and had spent all that she had, and was nothing bettered, but rather grew worse, When she had heard of Jesus, came in the press behind, and touched his garment. For she said, If I may touch but his clothes, I shall be whole. And straightway the fountain of her blood was dried up; and she felt in her body that she was healed of that plague. And Jesus, immediately knowing in himself that virtue had gone out of him, turned him about in the press, and said, Who touched my clothes?*

And his disciples said unto him, Thou seest the multitude thronging thee, and sayest thou, Who touched me? And he looked round about to see her that had done this thing. But the woman fearing and trembling, knowing what was done in her, came and fell down before him, and told him all the truth. And he said unto her, Daughter, thy faith hath made thee whole; go in peace, and be whole of thy plague." I believe that you have entered into a season when it is officially time for the hemorrhaging to stop in every area of your life. Many of you reading this have been bleeding with insecurities, disappointments, a religious spirit, unforgiveness, frustration, debt, sickness and disease, and you have been bleeding with too many false imaginations of who you are. It really doesn't matter where you have been bleeding because you have been bleeding in your heart for too long. IT'S TIME FOR THE BLEEDING TO STOP, IN JESUS NAME!

The scripture said that this woman had an issue of blood for 12 long years. I mentioned a portion of what the number 12 represents in an earlier chapter. However, here is a more in-depth look at what it means. The number 12 represents divine authority and appointment, as well as governmental foundation and perfection. It is the number that shows completion. In essence, the number 12 denotes an end of one thing and the beginning of something new. I will repeat that: the number 12 denotes an end of one thing and the beginning of something new. I see an end has come to one season and the beginning of another season has come.

In the book of II Chronicles 34:1-7, the scripture says, *"Josiah was eight years old when he began to reign, and he reigned in Jerusalem one and thirty years. And he did that which was right in the sight of the Lord, and walked in the ways of David his father, and declined neither to the right hand, nor to the left. For in the eighth year of his reign, which he was yet young, he began to seek after the God of David his father: and in the twelfth year he began to purge Judah and Jerusalem from the high places, and the groves, and the carved images, and the molten images. And they brake down the altars of Baalim in his presence; and the images, that were on high above them, he cut down; and the groves, and the carved images, and the molten images, he brake in pieces, and made dust of them, and strowed it upon the graves of them that had sacrificed unto them. And he burnt the bones of the priests upon their altars, and cleansed Judah and Jerusalem. And so did he in the cities of Manasseh, and Ephraim, and Simeon, even unto Naphtali, with their mattocks round about. And when he had broken down the altars and the groves, and had beaten the graven images into powder, and cut down all the idols throughout all the land of Israel, he returned to Jerusalem."* Josiah was eight (8) years old when he began to reign. The number 8 means new beginning. Josiah in the 8th year of his reign began seeking after the God of his father David. Josiah declined to do anything that would cause him to walk in error.

In the 12th year, Josiah began to purge both Judah and Jerusalem from the high places and the false, carved and molten images that would violate the image of the God he was pursuing. It is in the 12th year of school in the United States when there is a graduation or commencement exercise where the senior receives a diploma for successfully completing 12 years of school. Lord Jesus! The Spirit of the Lord said it's time to graduate from the elementary things of the kingdom and on to the mature things. It's time for the Word to purge any other image that would exalt itself against the wisdom and knowledge of God (II Corinthians 10:3-6). It's time for those things in you to be brought into captivity and submit to the obedience of Jesus Christ.

There was a reason why this woman with an issue of blood was hemorrhaging for 12 years and could not get healed after having many doctor visits. It's because they spent years treating the symptoms and not getting to the root cause of why she was bleeding in the first place. You need to know that there is a root to the branch. There is a root cause to the many "whys" and the Spirit of the Lord is coming after it today!

The scripture says in John 15:2, *"Every branch in me that*

beareth not fruit he taketh away: and every branch that beareth fruit, he purgeth it, that it may bring forth more fruit." God is coming after the very thing in this season that has caused you to be barren in certain areas of your life. He is coming after the thing that you refused to allow His Word to cut away at after 3 years. The scripture says in Luke 13:6-9 that after 3 years if it has no fruit upon the vine cut it down. You just read in John, Chapter 15, that every branch in God that has not birthed forth any fruit by now, God is saying, I the Lord thy God will not wink at it any more, I will take it away.

The woman with an issue of blood went to doctor after doctor for years looking for a physical healing with her issue of blood. But for years the doctors treated the symptoms instead of the root that caused that bleeding. In 12 years, no doctor was ever able to bring her to the place of healing because in the natural, treating the symptoms would only make someone feel better temporarily, with no permanent and eternal resolve. This is why you get those who come into the church, shout all over the place, wave their hands in the air, rejoice as the Word of God is going forth and then they leave out of the church unfulfilled. Why? It's because the praise and worship only treat the symptoms. The dancing all over the church only treats the symptoms. The affirmation from the pastor and first lady only treat the symptoms.

But only application of what you heard can begin a work in your heart that will renew the right spirit within you! A good physician will find out what the source of the problem is and where it is coming from. However, **many want an outside deliverance for an inside war.** The Great Physician is here with a diagnosis and an antidote if you will receive it and harden not your heart!

The scripture said that her symptoms only got worse. It got worse because this issue was not coming from external sources. She did not have a with-out problem, she had a **within** problem. This explains why what she had was untreatable by medicinal methods. Come in a little bit closer so that you can hear what I am saying to you by the Spirit. It's not them; IT'S YOU or better yet, ISS-UE!

You have people in the church, who are always in the middle of something. Every time you turn around they are in the midst of some mess and everybody else is the problem. I want to submit to you today that it's not them; again, ISS-UE! See the woman with the ISS-UE of blood did not have an extrinsic problem, but an intrinsic one. This explains why she had gone to many physicians, but her condition grew worse and she had spent all she had. Because it didn't matter what medicine they gave her, it was not feasible or conducive to heal heart failure. I have an announcement for you today that should set you free inwardly.

You can buy and wear Christian Loubitan, St. John and Tori Burch all day long. You can spend all of your money on you, but buying expensive things will only treat the symptoms. There is a reason why some, not all, have to garment themselves with hundreds of dollars' worth of garments because they feel less than a $1 on the inside. You cannot kill a grasshopper mentality with stuff or by the flesh. You must kill a grasshopper mentality by the Spirit!

The scripture says in the book of Colossians 3:1-3, *"If ye then be risen with Christ, seek those things which are above, where Christ sitteth on the right hand of God. Set your affection on things above, not on things on the earth. For ye are dead, and your life is hid with Christ in God."* See here's the truth: Salvation will only treat the symptoms, but pursuing God with your whole heart will get to the root cause of why you do what you do, react the way you react and feel the way you feel. How do I know? The scripture says in Jeremiah 17:9-10, *"The heart is deceitful above all things, and desperately wicked: who can know it? I the Lord search the heart, I try the reins, even to give every man according to his ways, and according to the fruit of his doings."* Only God can search out the heart. He is the only archaeologist that can excavate out of you what is not good for you. This is the year that God desires to rid you of your issues. However, you must acknowledge Him in all your ways. You must acknowledge that there is hurt there because of this or disappointment there because of that, so that the hemorrhaging can stop in Jesus name. Something is hindering your ability to produce and until you get past it, you will be barren in that area.

The scripture says in II Peter 1:8, *"For if these things be in you, and abound, they make you that ye shall neither be barren nor unfruitful in the knowledge of our Lord Jesus Christ."* Hear me by the Spirit when I say, something is not abounding. That word that you thought took root didn't. How do I know? In the book of Mark 4:3-9, 14, the scripture says, *"Hearken; Behold, there went out a sower to sow: And it came to pass, as he sowed, some fell by the way side, and the fowls of the air came and devoured it up. And some fell on stony ground, where it had not much earth; and immediately it sprang up, because it had no depth of earth: But when the sun was up, it was scorched; and because it had no root, it withered away. And some fell among thorns, and the thorns grew up and choked it, and it yielded no fruit. And other fell on good ground, and did yield fruit that sprang up and increased; and brought forth, some thirty, and some sixty, and some an hundred. And he said unto them, He that hath ears to hear, let him hear."* So here we find that dependent upon the soil in which the seed is sown into, will determine the kind of harvest that is obtained. The soil here is a direct representation of your heart. In verse 14, it clarifies what the sower is sowing. It says that the sower sows the Word!

In Hebrews 4:12, the scripture says, *"For the word of God is quick, and powerful, and sharper than any twoedged sword, piercing even to the dividing asunder of soul and spirit, and of the joints and marrow, and is a discerner of the thoughts and intents of the heart."* The scripture said that the sower sows the Word. Then Hebrews 4:12 says that the Word of God pierces and divides asunder both the soul and spirit. It also says that the Word is a discerner of the thoughts and intents of the heart. It is the Word of God that has the ability to discern the thoughts and the intents of a man's heart.

After reading Mark, Chapter 4, the conditions of the heart can be: 1) a fall by the wayside heart; 2) a stony ground heart; 3) a heart full of thorns; or 4) a good ground heart. **The condition of your heart will determine the outcome of your harvest.** It will determine the outcome of your decree. Oh my God in heaven alone! The scripture says in Isaiah 55:10-11, *"For as the rain cometh down, and the snow from heaven, and returneth not thither, but watereth the earth, and maketh it bring forth and bud, that it may give seed to the sower, and bread to the eater: So shall my word be that goeth forth out of my mouth: it shall not return unto me void, but it shall accomplish that which I please, and it shall* *prosper in the thing whereto I sent it."* Thus, I must repeat what I said earlier, something in the receptacle is not abounding because the Word is fruitful by itself. As a matter of fact, Daniel 2:44 says this, *"And in the days of these kings shall the God of heaven set up a kingdom, which shall never be destroyed: and the kingdom shall not be left to other people, but it shall break in pieces and consume all these kingdoms, and it shall stand for ever."* Anything in your heart that is not of God is considered another kingdom and God said there shall be no other kingdom that shall withstand the kingdom of God. According to this verse of scripture, He will consume those kingdoms into pieces or fragments. God will never contend with any other kingdom.

If you think about it, the scripture says in I John 3:8, *".....For this purpose the Son of God was manifested, that he might destroy the works of the devil."* The devil represents the kingdom of darkness. A kingdom could be described as anything that exalts itself against the wisdom and knowledge of God. All of this makes sense to me now. I believe when read by men and women alike, this chapter of the book will reach across borders and infect nations. For women, I believe it will cause us to get being the wailing women and not the warring against one another women. Because the only reason there is division in any relationship is because the heart has been divided from the Word of God. If a heart is not connected to God, it cannot effectively connect to people. Our hearts must be knit together in love with God, in order for it to be knit together in love with man.

As I was writing, the Spirit of the Lord spoke to me and said, "Healing must take place in the heart so that the miscarriages can stop." In the book of Hosea, Chapter 9 there is something you must see. However, let me set this up so that you will understand Hosea's frustration. In Hosea, Chapter 8, God was upset with Israel because they transgressed His covenant and trespassed His law by setting up kings that were not set up by God. They set up princes and the silver and gold they made into idols. So God was upset because of the disobedience in their heart and their disobedience affected their prayers for deliverance.

In the book of Hosea, Chapter 9, God punishes them because their hearts were far from the covenant and Hosea says that there will be no birth, no pregnancies and no conceptions. Then in Hosea 9:14, Hosea begins to pray an angry prayer against the people. The scripture says, *"Give them, O Lord: what wilt thou give? Give them a miscarrying womb and dry breasts."* He starts out by saying, *("Give them, O LORD")*. Then he stopped because he checked his heart and didn't know what to pray. This led him to say, *"What will you give?"* In the end, Hosea asked for a miscarrying womb and dry breasts. Really if you look at it,

Hosea was praying for mercy. He knew of the coming judgment, so he prayed "LORD, give them few children so those children will not have to face the dread of your coming judgment." What point am I making? The prophet Hosea asked that because of their disobedience, Lord give them miscarrying wombs.

I must provide clarity here so that in all your getting, you will get understanding. In the natural, when a woman miscarries during pregnancy, the first sign is bleeding. A miscarriage in the natural happens because there is some chromosomal abnormality that causes such a traumatic moment. In essence, something is wrong, or something is dysfunctional. Something did not connect. Thus, the semen from the man or the egg from the woman, one or the other didn't connect. Medically speaking, Dr. Bryan Cowan, Chair of the Department of Obstetrics and Gynecology at the University of Mississippi Medical Center said that mismatched chromosomes account for 60% of miscarriages. While this number provides explanation for more than half of the miscarriages that take place in the natural, I must make something prophetically clear in the spirit as it relates to our God. When the semen of His Word is released, the condition of your heart must be conducive to good ground in order for the promises of God to be released in your life. There lies your answer to the delay of your harvest in years past. What was the condition of your heart during that time?

The reason why many of you haven't given birth to that prophecy is because you could have very well had a miscarriage.

Many believers mis-carry the Word of God and blame it on God. However, the scripture says in I Samuel 16:7, *"....for man looketh on the outward appearance, but the Lord looketh on the heart."* When God looks at your heart, be honest with yourself and tell yourself what does He really see? Because based on what He sees this year, not what I see, not your pastors, not your friend, it will determine the fulfillment of the promise, and the fulfillment of the prophecy. Hear me clearly by the Spirit when I say, IT'S TIME FOR THE HEMORRHAGING TO STOP!

In the book of Matthew 23:26-28, the scripture says, *"Thou blind Pharisee, cleanse first that which is within the cup and platter, that the outside of them may be clean also. Woe unto you, scribes and Pharisees, hypocrites! for ye are like unto whited sephulcres, which indeed appear beautiful outward, but are within full of dead men's bones, and of all uncleanness. Even so ye also outwardly appear righteous unto men, but within ye are full of hypocrisy and iniquity."* Many clean up outwardly really well, but sometimes it's a cover up for really what's going on the inside. There is no need for me to tiptoe around the truth. Not to include, as a joint-heir and co-laborer with Christ my assignment in the earth is to expose every lie and defy the works of darkness by executing the agenda of the kingdom of God. Therefore, I will say that too much is riding on your complete deliverance and you must know the truth because the truth will make you free (John 8:32). Too many people are lying in the valley of decision awaiting your arrival.

It is imperative that you understand that you don't have time to pretend everything is okay anymore. Your vulnerability unto God is more important than you being vulnerable with others. The scripture says in John, Chapter 4, they that worship Him MUST worship Him in spirit and in truth. What point am I making? NOW IT'S TIME TO CLEAN THE INSIDE OF THE CUP, so that your cup can run over with glory and not grief. It's time to clean the inside of the cup, so that your cup can run over with peace and not pride. It's time to clean the inside of the cup so that your cup can run over with increase and not insecurities. Hear what the Spirit of the Lord is saying: IT'S TIME TO CLEAN THE INSIDE OF THE CUP PEOPLE OF GOD and annihilate every religious spirit!

The scripture says in the book of Mark 7:18-23, *"....Do ye not perceive, that whatsoever thing from without entereth into the man, it cannot defile him; Because it entereth not into his heart, but into the belly, and goeth out into the draught, purging all meats? And he said, That which cometh out of the man, that defileth the man. For from within out of the heart of men, proceed evil thoughts, adulteries, fornications, murders, Thefts, covetousness, wickedness, deceit, lasciviousness, an evil eye, blasphemy, pride, foolishness: All these evil things come from within, and defile the man."* So this woman with an issue of blood had a within problem not a without problem. The problem she was facing externally was a direct manifestation from what was happening within. She lacked healing because she lacked in her heart, not in the other parts of her body. God I know what I am talking about. The Lord said, "Daughter the main reason why you were barren in the natural was because your heart was barren. Thus, a barren and stony heart will produce a barren womb."

I had gone to many doctors and they all had the same diagnosis, "Mrs. Howard, you are sterile and unable to have children." Hear me clearly by the Spirit: there is no prescription for spiritual heart failure. They didn't have a natural cure for the place where I was bleeding. They didn't know that there was a root cause to the problem. They couldn't find it. Why? A heart that is infiltrated with unforgiveness cannot be detected on any medical cat-scan, ultrasound or MRI. Resentment cannot be detected. It is without a doubt, undetectable.

The doctors couldn't see the aftermath or the pain that was left after the molestation. They couldn't see the betrayal. They couldn't see the hurt. They couldn't see that I was wounded. They didn't know that what they were looking for was lying deep beneath the surface of my heart and it was undetectable. I had gone to many physicians, but neglected the Great Physician, Jesus Christ, who was able to stop me from bleeding immediately. There is a conversation happening in your heart right now with the Spirit of the Living God and you must yield to the spiritual diagnosis of heart failure to be healed, in Jesus Name. Something glorious is happening in you and you can no longer resist the continual touching of the hem of His garment. Be healed, be whole and be set free, in Jesus Name.

The scripture says in Proverbs 4:23, *"Keep thy heart with all diligence; for out of it are the issues of life."* Out of the heart flow the issues of life. I will repeat what I heard my husband, Pastor Derek say once during a service. He said, "The body of Christ does not have a gift or talent problem. The body of Christ has a heart problem." I must say, he was absolutely right. What was happening within the woman with an issue of blood, now affected her ability to be normal. Bleeding every day for 12 years or 4,384 days is not normal. This woman lived in a vicious cycle for 12 long years, bleeding and didn't die. Some of you should be dead by now according to the enemies score, but God was waiting until you got to the 12th year, like the woman with an issue of blood so that you could touch Him and the bleeding would cease immediately. The cycle had to end in her life and I decree and declare that the cycle will end today in yours.

Let me say this: A woman who had an issue of blood was considered unclean and according to the book of Leviticus 15:19-33, she was not supposed to be amongst the crowd. The scripture says she was supposed to be put away for seven days, but on the eighth day she was supposed to take a sin offering and a burnt offering to the priest and the priest would make an atonement for her. The word is *atone* means to cover. See the blood of bulls and goats would only cover the sin in the Old Testament. It did not eradicate the sin.

When Jesus shed His blood, the scripture said in the book of Hebrews, Chapter 9, verse 12, that He entered in ONCE into the holy place and obtained eternal redemption for us. This woman had been bleeding for 12 years. But when she touched the hem of His garment, she touched eternal redemption, the sin was eradicated and immediately she was made whole. God allowed her to be in an impossible situation so that she could see that all things are possible to those who believe in their heart. Some of you reading this book are in impossible situations and God said, according to the book of John 11:4, this sickness is not unto death, but for the glory of God, that the Son of God might be glorified thereby. Touch Him with your heart and your body will be healed of whatever has caused you dis-ease.

This woman was supposed to be isolated and not among others until her issue of blood had dried up. Well I began this interrogation to the Holy Spirit asking: What was she doing amongst the multitude? What led her to bypass what was traditional and the law to move into the crowds to get to Jesus – the law breaker? Listen to me women of God. This woman with an issue of blood was amongst the multitude and amongst the crowd because she wasn't the only one who had an issue. She was amongst a whole crowd of people that had issues. She was not the only somebody that was bleeding, and she was not the only somebody who had something going on from within. She was in the multitude because everybody had an issue of something.

When I think about Jesus, I can only reflect upon how he did everything outside of the systems of this world. He did a great work outside of every system you could ever name: the religious, political, educational, and every other system that is considered to be a combination of things or parts forming a complex or unitary whole. You name it and He did a work outside of that system. If you think about it, nobody hated Jesus more than the church people. Jesus was more controversial and contentious to religious people more than He was with those who were secular. It was the

Pharisees and the Sadducees and the church people who were always trying to kill Him. He worked outside of the system. He was born outside of the system. The greatest birth in history took place in a barn, a rather obscure place; a place totally outside of the world systems. Jesus even died outside of the system.

The scripture says in the book of Hebrews 13:12, in the New Living Translation, *"So also Jesus suffered and died outside the city gates to make his people holy by means of his own blood."* He died outside of the gates of Jerusalem. They rejected Him and shut the gate on him. In that place, the place called Golgotha is where Jesus hung his head and stretched himself wide for all to see. He died outside of the system so that all of us who would ever be rejected outside of the system would have an opportunity to be able to conquer it. If you have ever been rejected, don't worry, it is evidence that like Jesus, you have an outside-of-the-system anointing that will cause breakthrough in the realm of the unseen.

So for Jesus to be in the midst of the people, in the book of Mark, Chapter 5, with issues wasn't uncommon. He positioned her and all the others to do one thing and that is to touch the hem of His garment. Why didn't she touch his sleeve? Why didn't she touch His hand? There are many reasons, but I will only discuss a few.

During any natural menstrual cycle which can go from 3 –

7 days, most women are wearied and tired in their body. So can you imagine bleeding for 12 uninterrupted years? She had to be very weary. In the book of I Samuel, Chapter 24, I found a fascinating truth that the Spirit of the Lord revealed. The scripture says in I Samuel 24:4-6, *"And the men of David said unto him, Behold the day of which the Lord said unto thee, Behold, I will deliver thine enemy into thine hand, that thou mayest do to him as it shall seem good unto thee. Then David arose, and cut off the skirt of Saul's robe privily. And it came to pass afterward, that David's heart smote him, because he had cut off Saul's skirt. And he said unto his men, The Lord forbid that I should do this thing unto my master, the Lord's anointed, to stretch forth mine hand against him, seeing he is the anointed of the Lord."* David cut off the skirt of Saul's robe. In laymen's terms, he cut off Saul's hem on his robe. David was grieved in his heart because cutting off Saul's hem represented him cutting away at Saul's authority.

When the woman with an issue of blood touched the hem of Jesus' garment, she touched the authority of Jesus Christ and was made whole. Why? In the book of Matthew 14:35-36, the scripture says, *"...People brought all their sick to him and begged him to let the sick just touch the edge of His cloak, and all who touched Him were healed."* Then the scripture says this in Matthew 22:37-40, *"Jesus said unto him, Thou shalt love the Lord thy God with all thy heart, and with all thy soul, and with all thy mind. This is the first and great commandment. And the second is like unto it, Thou shalt love thy neighbor as thyself. On these two commandments hang all the law and the prophets."* The scripture instructed us to love the Lord thy God with all our heart, soul and mind. Then it said that on these two commandments hang all the law and the prophets.

When the woman with an issue of blood touched the hem of His garment, **she touched the law and the fulfillment of prophecy at the same time.** Jesus came to fulfill the law and the scripture says in Revelation 19:10, *"...for the testimony of Jesus is the spirit of prophecy."* She touched the law and prophecy at the same time, which is why what she did caused virtue or power to leave from Him. This is what would happen on Calvary, the law and the prophecy would be fulfilled when He would declare that IT IS FINISHED and give up the Ghost. Virtue (power) would leave Him, because He would need that power, the Holy Ghost to raise Him up on the 3rd day! I decree and declare that when you touch Him this time....IT IS FINISHED!

She was the only one who touched Him because she was the only one who was willing to acknowledge that she had an issue. She knew that He was her only pathway to complete deliverance. The devil is a liar when he tells you that you are the only somebody with an issue. You are not the only somebody going through that situation. There are others, but they are too afraid to touch him because they don't want others to know they are going through. Contrary to popular and your most holier than thou belief, EVERYONE HAS AN ISSUE OF SOMETHING!

Let me explain to you further the release of power behind her touching the hem of Jesus' garment. In my study time, I discovered that the word **hem** means, *tassel, fringe, or the border of a garment.* In the book of Numbers 15:38, the scripture says, *"Speak unto the children of Israel, and bid them that they* **make them fringes in the borders of their garments** *throughout their generations, and that they put upon the fringe of the borders a ribband of blue."* The word *fringe* means the same thing as the word *hem* in the book of Matthew 9:20-22 and Matthew 14:36. It is the Hebrew word "***Tzitzit***" and it speaks of a "***tassel***".

The Jews wore tassels on their garments as a continuous reminder of their relationship to the Lord. There were tassels on the four corners of their garments to remind the ancient Jews that they were required to obey the Lord. It did not matter in what direction they turned; they would see the tassels and be instantly reminded of their obligation to keep the Lord's commandments.

When we think of the commandments, we always think there are only Ten Commandments based upon what most of us have read in the book of Exodus, Chapter 20. This is why we have to study to show ourselves approved. The Jewish rabbis identified 613 commandments in the Torah, which are the first five books of the bible (Genesis, Exodus, Leviticus, Numbers and Deuteronomy). There were 365 *"Thou shalt nots"* and 248 *"Thou shalts"*. The tassels on the borders or hem of their garments were a constant reminder of their responsibility to keep the Law and not turn away from it to the right or to the left. Again, when this woman with an issue of blood touched the hem of His garment she touched the law and the fulfillment of prophecy at the same time. It's your time to touch Him so that the Word of God can be fulfilled in your life.

The scripture says in Psalm 138:8, that the Lord will perfect that which concerns you. You cannot perfect the imperfections in your heart. GOD HAS TO PERFECT THAT WHICH CONCERNS YOU! However, you have to be like this woman and press pass others with their issues to get to Jesus who is able to stop you from bleeding and heal you everywhere you hurt. I am assured that because this woman was bleeding for 12 years, she had other unmentionable issues that were birthed out of the initial issue of blood. When you refuse to deal with the little foxes found in the book of Solomon 2:15, they have the potential to turn into a BIG BAD WOLF and spoil the entire vine! Tommy

Tenney says in his book entitled, <u>Finding Favor with the King</u>, "What you don't eradicate when you are strong will come back to attack you when you are weak." Worse than that if you don't deal with your inner-me now, your children will have to deal with your inner-me's tomorrow. In essence, kill Goliath now or it will birth out babies in your bloodline.

I began thinking; it took this woman 12 years to get up enough nerve to acknowledge that she had an issue. I must utilize this space to speak to women. How long will it take you to simply acknowledge that there is something going on in you? When will you acknowledge that you have an issue in a certain area of your life? When will you stop tricking yourself out of your own deliverance? When will you simply admit to being insecure? When will you admit that you lack confidence, have self-esteem issues, and don't like it when others are promoted before you because you are used to winning? When will you yield to the truth about you and admit that you have a real problem submitting to authority? Some of you reading this refuse to submit to the anointing in someone else's life because you don't feel that they are as anointed as you are.

Many of you won't get too close to people because you think they might hurt you, betray you, or disappoint you. I have counseled many women and have discovered that the reason why they cannot be happy for others is because they are really not happy with themselves. Some are even terrified to be by themselves, fearful of what they will discover about their individual selves. You are bleeding woman of God.

Despite how many women in your family had the same conversation with themselves, I know what it's like carrying the residue of soul-ties for years. I know what it's like dealing with the aftermath of an abortion for 20 years. I know what it's like being tormented by molestation for 18 years. I know how painful some secrets can be as quiet as they are kept. I know what it's like for you to watch your friends and family members get pregnant when you are barren because of the poor choices. These are traits of a woman with an issue of blood. The only way the bleeding will ever stop is to acknowledge them before the Lord. I told you it doesn't matter what you cover it up with or who you cover it up with, none of it can cover up the fragmented frustration in your heart!

I heard something before finishing this chapter that I know will set every captive in you free. I have read this scripture a million times. However, I have never seen it in the way God revealed it one night. God used Apostle Jerome Cade mightily at the annual F.R.E.E. (Fully Restored Empowered and Encouraged) Conference at Church of the Living Way in January, 2012 to reveal to us a more excellent way. The scripture says in Genesis 41:50-52, *"And unto Joseph were born two sons before the years of famine came, which Asenath the daughter of Potipherah priest of On bare unto him. And Joseph called the name of the firstborn Manasseh: For God, said he, hath made me forget all my toil, and all my father's house. And the name of the second called he Ephraim: For God hath caused me to be fruitful in the land of my affliction."* The first born son's name was Manasseh, whose name means "to forget". The second born was Ephraim, whose name means "double-fruit".

God said to me that there will be multiple births that will take place in the lives of those who read this book and receive the instructions from the heart of God. Many would ask, "How shall this be?" The Spirit of the Living God is going to cause you to forget and have double-fruit in the land where you have experienced the most pain. God is going to give each of you a Manasseh experience and an Ephraim experience. However, one is a prerequisite of the other.

You must **forget** those things that are behind before you can see the double fruit that is before you. Apostle Cade told many who were at the conference that Sunday night, that a Manasseh experience will not erase the memory but will annihilate the misery. My prayer is that you will have a Manasseh experience while you are reading this chapter, in Jesus name.

You have to know and understand why forgetting is so important in the life of the believer. The enemy knows the Word of God better than some believers and he uses what you should know against you. Several years ago, I stood over my grandmother's casket preaching at her Home going service. This was a very painful and what I thought unforgettable moment in my life. Well the doctors said that this dis-ease called Alzheimer's is what led her to the end of her life here in the earth. While she was alive, I would spend hours doing research on this disease because I was convinced that she would be the first testimony in the earth where God supernaturally healed someone.

Well in my time of studying, I discovered something vitally important. Alzheimer's is a type of dementia that causes problems with memory, thinking and behavior. One part of the brain breaks down and starts to fail. Hear me clearly by the Spirit. Here lies the problem with the people in the church. We believe that because we have accepted Jesus as Lord, everything about our lives has already been covered and dealt with because of the blood of Jesus. Wrong? While your spirit man is immediately saved, the saving of your soul which encompasses your mind, human will and emotions is a day to day process.

The scripture says in I Thessalonians 5:23, *"And the very*

God of peace sanctify you wholly; and I pray God your whole spirit and soul and body be preserved blameless unto the coming of our Lord Jesus Christ." God desires that you are sanctified WHOLLY. This includes, spirit, soul and body. Thus, I know this is not something that is practiced in the "church" circuit but it's the truth. We are a very imbalanced people. We think that going to a psychiatrist is bad. I believe you need both spiritual and natural counseling if you are going to be sanctified WHOLLY.

The scripture says in Proverbs 11:1, *"A false balance is abomination to the Lord: but a just weight is his delight."* God desires for the body of Christ to be a just weight, not an imbalanced organism. Whatever needs to happen for you to mature and grow in God WHOLLY, you must do it. If you don't, you will never have an Ephraim experience if you don't have a Manasseh experience and forget those things which are behind. I honestly believe the enemy is wicked and if you don't have a Manasseh experience and forget voluntarily, the enemy will try to use it against you with an Alzheimer experience and cause you to forget involuntarily. This is why the Word of God says that God throws our sins in the sea of forgetfulness in the book of Micah 7:19. God doesn't remember your past and neither should you.

The scripture say in Isaiah 43:18-19, *"Remember ye not the former things, neither consider the things of old. Behold, I will do a new thing; now it shall spring forth; shall ye not know it? I will even make a way in the wilderness, and rivers in the desert."* God is ready to do a new thing and now it shall spring forth! What is the new thing? God desires to create in you a clean heart and RENEW the right spirit within you! It's time to get out of the crowd and press pass the multitude and get to the God who is able to heal you from within. It's time for you to change your posture. It's the posture of faith that will cause virtue to leave out of Him. It's time for the hemorrhaging to stop NOW IN JESUS NAME!

Chapter 3: The Choice: "Are You Willing to Carry the Baby Full Term"

"The Choice: Are You Willing to Carry The Baby Full-Term"

I must first ask you the question the Lord asked me. *"Are You Willing to Carry the Baby Full Term-In Spite of How Much It May Cost You?"* I am going to repeat that again just for the purpose of your natural eyes, to make sure that you have divine understanding of that which the Lord is asking of you. *"Are You Willing to Carry the Baby Full Term-In Spite of How Much It May Cost You?"* What I found while on my Christian journey is that just like it is in the natural, you cannot get pregnant in the realm of the Spirit unless you have intercourse. The Spirit of the Living God instructed me to stay in my lane with this book and minister where my anointing lies. Out of experience and endurance by faith, my anointing lies in the area of **spiritual intercourse, conception, and delivery**. God's intent with this book is to make sure you know not only what it is you're carrying, but also to ask you *"Are You Willing to Carry the Baby Full Term-In Spite of How Much It May Cost You?"*

The first step in the birthing process begins with a decision. The decision involves more than a simple yes. This decision will determine your next move. The decision will include whether or not you will receive the semen of His Word, will you mis-carry or will you destroy the seed by means of spiritual abortion, or will you agree with God and carry the "baby" full term. Many of us have never looked at the Word of God in this manner. However, every spiritual analogy has a natural parallel. I know many of you are saying what does spiritual intercourse, conception and delivery really mean? **Spiritual conceptions** take place when there is **spiritual intercourse**. It is the only way I know how to get pregnant in the realm of the Spirit. **Spiritual intercourse** is that level of intimacy with God where His seed, His Word is released within your Spirit – your Spirit is like the womb of a woman. The seed is planted during prayer, reading the Word and every time there is a two-way communication between you and God. Once a seed is planted in your spirit, if it receives the proper nourishment, the seed will grow and **God will deliver it**.

When God plants anything, He will deliver it, because it was not man conceived. It is the same way the Spirit of the Lord came upon Mary and impregnated her with Jesus Christ. When you are intimate with God, the semen of His Word will cause a conception to take place within your spirit man that can only be aborted by lack of nourishment by the Word of God. It will live and not die and provide the manifestation that was purposed by the Father. You must make this declaration right now. Read it aloud: *"The seed was planted by God, I received divine substance from the Word of God; therefore I shall see the end that has been predestined – In Jesus Name!!*

What is it that you identify as your baby? Is it the vision God gave you about a ministry, about your family, about your health, about your finances? Whatever it is, the Lord said to ask you *"Are You Willing to Carry the Baby Full Term-In Spite of How Much It May Cost You?"* If you haven't noticed it yet, when you said "yes" to whatever the baby is, the enemy launched an attack in every area of your life.

In the book of Luke 1:26-38, the scripture says, *"And in the sixth month the angel Gabriel was sent from God unto a city of Galilee, named Nazareth, To a virgin espoused to a man whose name was Joseph, of the house of David; and the virgin's name was Mary. And the angel came in unto her, and said, Hail, thou that art highly favoured, the Lord is with thee: blessed art thou among women. And when she saw him, she was troubled at his saying, and cast in her mind what manner of salutation this should be. And the angel said unto her, Fear not, Mary: for thou hast found favour with God. And, behold, thou shalt conceive in thy womb, and bring forth a son, and shalt call his name JESUS. He shall be great, and shall be called the Son of the Highest: and the Lord God shall give unto him the throne of his father David: And he shall reign over the house of Jacob for ever; and of his kingdom there shall be no end. Then said Mary unto the angel, How shall this be, seeing I know not a man? And the angel answered and said unto her, The Holy Ghost shall come upon thee, and the power of the Highest shall overshadow thee: therefore also that holy thing which shall be born of thee shall be called the Son of God. And, behold, thy cousin Elisabeth, she hath also conceived a son in her old age: and this is the sixth month with her, who was called barren. For with God nothing shall be impossible. And Mary said, Behold the handmaid of the Lord; be it unto me according to thy word. And the angel departed from her."* I began to wonder, why Mary would say "yes" to carry something that would cause change in every area of her life. Why would she open herself up to ridicule, embarrassment, humiliation, disappointment, and all the pains that would be associated with carrying this baby? Is there anyone reading this who knows what I am talking about by the Spirit? Why would she agree to the weight that this assignment would bring?

    The Spirit of the Lord made it clear to me. Mary agreed so that she could see the fullness of God and the kingdom of God come through her. What point am I making? The only reason why God told you to do that "thing", that business, that ministry, whatever it is He told you to do is so that the kingdom could come through you. His desire is for His will to be done on earth, as it is in heaven.

Believers need to get a grasp on kingdom realities. Jesus needs a body in the earth to carry out His divine plan. You and I are it. We are carriers of the glory and by-products of the kingdom of God on earth. Where has God instructed the kingdom in you to go? What has He instructed the kingdom in you to do? Whatever it is, you must avail yourself to that assignment. Yet, you must understand that when you say yes, there is a cost associated with it. Are you willing to submit to the payment and allow the deeds of your members to be mortified so that a God-ordained delivery can take place?

The scripture says in I Thessalonians 3:3, *"That no man should be moved by these afflictions: for yourselves know that we are appointed thereunto."* Can you endure what carrying this baby might cost you? Every mother in the natural has to pay their own individual price for each child they have ever carried. Some payments are more intense than others. As the baby grows, that woman becomes more uncomfortable and even irritable. More importantly, a natural pregnancy has 3 trimesters and with each trimester comes challenges. What am I saying? Dependent upon what trimester you're in will determine your weariness. Yet, you can't faint too early. You cannot abort spiritually or naturally. This spiritual delivery will change lives, including your own.

In Jeremiah12:5, the scripture says, *"If thou hast run with the footmen, and they have wearied thee, then how canst thou contend with horses? and if in the land of peace, wherein thou trustedst, they wearied thee, then how wilt thou do in the swelling of Jordan?"*. What is the Lord saying to you in these verses of scripture? It is very clear. If you can't handle the opposition in the first trimester, then you definitely will not be able to handle that which will come in the third trimester. Don't faint too early. You could risk putting the baby in danger, the vision and the ministry. Don't faint! God said you are doing well. Don't be weary in well doing, for you will reap, you will see the manifestation of that in which He planted if you faint not!

The Lord showed me that there were many of you that were on the verge of spiritual miscarriages. There are even many of you who were on the verge of spiritual abortions because of the many forces that have come to hinder the delivery. I kept hearing a voice the other day saying ABORT! ABORT! ABORT! The scripture says in John 10:4-5, *"......and the sheep follow him: for they know his voice. And a stranger will they not follow...."* I knew it wasn't the voice of God. The enemy is after the vision and the prophecy. He is after what God promised you in prayer – DON'T ABORT!

You must know that no one can take your baby or promise that God made to you. You must ABORT IT – DON'T ABORT! In Luke 1:28, the scripture says, *"And the angel came in unto her, and said, Hail, thou that art highly favoured, the Lord is with thee: blessed art thou among women."* The angel of the Lord basically said to Mary and God is saying to you today: Now before you reply regarding that in which I shall transport through you, you need to know that **the favor of the Lord is upon you to carry this baby**, to carry this vision, to carry this prophecy. What is favor? It is preferential treatment, unfair partiality and the state of being approved; it means to prefer. **God preferred you over others to carry out this assignment**, because you are special to God. It didn't matter about Mary's past. She had connected with the true vine, which caused a supernatural conception.

This conception would bring forth the greatest sacrifice ever made, Jesus Christ. It doesn't matter about your past. It was an exit God used to get you into your present. REJOICE, you have been favored by God to carry this baby and at the appointed time in the kingdom you will deliver it in its fullness. As a matter of fact, God has sent some Elisabeth's before you, who have done the very thing God has instructed you to do. An "Elisabeth" will be instrumental in pushing you into the place of destiny that God has purposed. Keep your Spirit open for your "Elisabeth", she is already in the earth, looking to connect and help you move toward the fulfillment of the promises of God.

It became very clear to me after reading this passage of

scripture repetitiously that the Lord impregnated Elisabeth for Mary. Mary needed someone to go before her to make every crooked place straight and every rough place plain. Mary needed a midwife. My favorite verse is in Luke 1:34. The scripture says, *"Then said Mary unto the angel, How shall this be, seeing I know not a man?"* Mary said now God how can this be, I don't have a man to impregnate me. Some of you who are reading this at this very moment are saying Lord, "how can this be when I don't have all the resources necessary to carry this thing?"

I mentioned to you earlier that the Lord impregnated Elisabeth for Mary. The Lord knew that Mary would ask the question, *"Lord how shall this be done?"* We must always remember that before we call unto our God, He has already provided an answer with evidence. The angel of the Lord replied and told Mary, and I am paraphrasing, "An answer has already been released in your cousin Elisabeth, the one who was barren, she is already six months pregnant". Now the answer to your question should be very clear, God is going to do it. He did it for Elisabeth!

When He wants to impregnate you with His fullness, He will come in unto you through and by the manifestation of His power – the Holy Ghost!" Today you must hear your God clearly. In the natural, invitro-fertilization is an abnormal way to impregnate a woman. God is saying to you, you didn't conceive this baby like those in the world. This was an abnormal, supernatural conception. Therefore, you must know that you don't need a man, you need God. You don't need all the money you think you need, you need God and His favor that He spoke at the beginning. You don't need 30 more people to accomplish the assignment; you need the Spirit beyond measure. What God has given you shall be taken care of by the one who planted it – the Almighty God.

According to Zechariah 4:6, it shall *"....Not by might, nor by power, but by my spirit, saith the Lord of hosts."* Whatever it is you lack will not hinder the growth and development of the baby or the vision. However, any disconnect from the true vine in John, Chapter 15 will hinder its growth. You must remain connected to the "Giver of Life" to see the full manifestation of what He planted. It was His seed and He will bring the increase.

The opposition and the resistance is not because of your name, your title, or who you are in the ministry - NO. It is because of the seed that was planted and its power to reproduce again. I say to people all the time, because I am connected to Christ Jesus, I am always giving birth to something. You're life and mine was never meant to be barren. It is simply because God's desire is for us to be fruitful. However, one of the key elements is found in II

Peter 1:8, which says, *"For if these things be in you, and abound, they make you that ye shall neither be barren nor unfruitful in the knowledge of our Lord Jesus Christ."* If the Word of God is consistently being applied within you, you shall never be barren. Neither shall you worry about whether you can carry the baby that He has placed within your Spirit, because of your connection to the umbilical cord of life – Jesus Christ!

In Isaiah 62:4, the scripture says, *"Thou shalt no more be termed Forsaken; neither shall thy land any more be termed Desolate: but thou shalt be called Hephzibah, and thy land Beulah: for the Lord delighteth in thee, and thy land shall be married."* God is simply saying, you shall no more be termed barren, forsaken or desolate; but a marriage is scheduled to take place. The marriage will be between what God sees and has promised with that in which you have decreed on purpose! A marriage is between the unseen and the seen are scheduled to meet and have a head on collision in your life. The tangible and the intangible have an appointment. When the two meet, what is tangible will overtake the intangible. This book is a tangible manifestation of what God promised. It is evidence and the divine connection ordained by God to ensure that you carry this baby full term.

If you ask any woman that has gone through more than one

pregnancy, she will tell you that all pregnancies are different. My first pregnancy was totally effortless; but the second one was on another level and I couldn't use the same strategies as before. What am I saying? You may have been able to push past the opposition to deliver the last time; but this time God has sent midwives who may have to help you take this one by force! According to Luke 1:45, the scripture says, *"And blessed is she that believed: for there shall be a performance of those things which were told her from the Lord."* I decree and declare that a performance and a display of God's favor will visit you! All you have to do is believe the Word of the Lord and decree the Word of the Lord, which will kill your doubts and release you to be fruitful and multiply in every area of your life!

Chapter 4: D.I.E. (Decrease in Everything)

"D.I.E. (Decrease In Everything)"

The agony and pain Jesus experienced at Calvary is symbolic of our walk on earth, as we endure our personal valleys through the shadow of death. As believers we sometimes tend to believe that suffering is not a part of our agreement with Christ. We think of it as punishment for our sins. However, I beg to differ. According to Hebrews 4:15, Jesus Christ, the Son of the living God, a godly seed, who was *without sin*, was spit upon, nailed to the cross, shed His Blood and willed Himself to die. He didn't suffer because He was being punished. He yielded Himself to the suffering because he understood a greater good would follow; and out of His death greatness would be birthed and many would follow.

In I Peter 1:11, the scripture says, *"Searching what, or what manner of time the Spirit of Christ which was in them did signify, when it testified beforehand the sufferings of Christ, and the glory that should follow."* The scripture says in Romans 8:18, *"For I reckon that the sufferings of this present time are not worthy to be compared with the glory which shall be revealed in us."* The sufferings that you will, or have experienced, are no comparison to the glory that will come forth out of the suffering. Therefore, for those of you who are reading this right at this very moment, you have not suffered for nothing. I am not telling you about something I heard, but what I know from experience. You were sentenced to death so that the glory of the Lord could be revealed in your life. Your life has been patterned after the ultimate sacrifice of Jesus Christ. The scripture says in II Timothy 3:12, *"Yea, and all that will live godly in Christ Jesus will suffer persecution."* When you and I said "yes" to Christ, we also agreed to D.I.E. (**D**ecrease **I**n **E**verything)!

As a member of the commonwealth society of the kingdom of God, you are entitled to many things. You are entitled to healing, salvation for your loved ones, peace, joy, prosperity, happiness and the fullness that the kingdom has to offer. You are a joint-heir with Christ. Therefore, your membership has its privileges. In essence, your connection to Christ has many benefits. But there is one very important element that you cannot escape. One of which entitles you to such benefits. As a matter of fact, it is a prerequisite based on the journey bestowed upon Christ. In order for you to live the abundant life that has been promised by Christ Jesus, you must be made aware that you are also going to have to walk through the valley of the shadow of death.

The scripture says in Psalm 23:4, *"Yea, though I walk through the valley of the shadow of death, I will fear no evil: for thou art with me; thy rod and thy staff they comfort me."* As a part of your covenant agreement with the entire kingdom of God, your walk with Christ requires that you mortify your body. The word *mortify* means to discipline one's body and physical appetites by self-denial or self-inflicted privation. The scripture says in Romans 8:13, *"For if ye live after the flesh, ye shall die: but if ye through the Spirit do mortify the deeds of the body, ye shall live."* In Colossians 3:5, the scripture says in the New Living translation, *"So put to death the sinful, earthly things lurking within you."* In essence, you must allow the Word of God to put to death everything that has the potential to exalt itself against the wisdom and knowledge of God.

I understand why Paul said in the book of I Corinthians 15:31 that he had to die daily. Obtaining godly discipline requires a consistent death of the flesh. Which means you must will yourself to die consistently to your way of doing things and live to the kingdom way of doing things. This is the only way to live if you desire to see the fullness of the kingdom and give birth to fruitful results.

In the book of Romans 6:16, the scripture says, *"Know ye not, that to whom ye yield yourselves servants to obey, his servants ye are to whom ye obey; whether of sin unto death, or of obedience unto righteousness?"* In essence, whether it be your Spirit man or your flesh, whichever you surrender yourself in obedience to, is the one who will have sovereign rule in your life. Surrendering to your Spirit man means you must be continually sanctified and cleansed by the Word of God daily.

The scripture says in Hebrews 4:12, *"For the word of God is quick, and powerful, and sharper than any two-edged sword, piercing even to the dividing asunder of soul and spirit, and of the joints and marrow, and is a discerner of the thoughts and intents of the heart."* As difficult as it may be, as a member of the Body of Christ, you must allow every part of you that would hinder your movement in the kingdom of God to be put to death with the Word of God.

The scripture says in the book of Philippians 2:8, *"And being found in fashion as a man, he humbled himself, and became obedient unto death, even the death of the cross."* Christ willed himself to die, because He knew that out of His death, lives would spring forth eternal. The scripture says in Romans 5:19, *"For as by one man's disobedience many were made sinners, so by the obedience of one shall many be made righteous."* Christ was sentenced to death so that you and I could live. God allowed His only begotten Son to be sentenced to death so that the will of God would be made manifest in the earth. How does this apply to you today? In II Timothy 2:10-12 in the New Living translation, Timothy said, *"I am willing to endure anything if it will bring salvation and eternal glory in Christ Jesus to those God has chosen. This is a true saying: If we die with him, we will also live with him. If we endure hardship, we will reign with him.....*" Timothy was willing to endure the cross and all of his misfortunes so that someone else could be saved. What a strong statement. However, it is the epitome of the life of Jesus Christ. Therefore, since He is our example, we must be willing to follow Him and do what He did, no matter the cost. We must realize that out of every death experience that we will ever face, life will spring forth for someone else.

I sometimes reflect back to the time when I was a young girl. I would have never believed that all of my life's experiences would be used for the glory of God. When I was 17, I contracted a venereal disease while involved in a promiscuous relationship. We will discuss more of this in a later chapter but I must lay this foundation. Little did I know that this venereal disease contraction would be the main attraction in my life that would lead me to Jesus Christ. The doctor's diagnosed me with Chlamydia, which was so bad, it birthed sterility. Sterility is the medical verbiage for a woman's inability to have children. Therefore, I had no other option but to give up my life of pleasing my flesh and pick up the life that God promised He would give me. But first, I had to turn from my wicked ways. In doing so, the embarrassment and humiliation of contracting a venereal disease and not being able to conceive became the weapon, the catalyst, and the platform that God would use to set many other young women free.

The scripture says in Revelation 12:11, *"...And they overcame him by the blood of the Lamb, and by the word of their testimony; and they loved not their lives unto the death."* Although I lost something because of my will to choose a moment of pleasure, I gained so much in return when I yielded myself to Christ way of doing things. Our death experiences birth testimonies that will not only bring glory to God, but will encourage someone else who may be on the verge of giving up or experiencing the same challenge. We must endure the death and the burial to experience the resurrection.

The scripture says in II Corinthians 4:17 in the New Living translation, *"For our present troubles are quite small and won't last very long. Yet they produce for us an immeasurably great glory that will last forever."* Every affliction or present trouble that has occurred in your life, though it may seem like it lasted for a lifetime, only lasted for a moment to provide a glory that will last eternally. Now I understand why it said in I Thessalonians 3:3, that for these afflictions were we appointed. Because although according to Psalm 34:19, the Lord will deliver you out of all your afflictions, He will allow your circumstances to generate the pain required for you to give birth to your greatest potential. Wow, what a word of healing for someone!

According to Colossians 1:27, the greatest potential found in every Believer is Christ, the hope of glory. Therefore, your death experience will reveal the treasure that is within your earthen vessel. You will never see the real you in Christ Jesus until you die! The power of Christ wasn't revealed until after He had died. For it is appointed unto a man to die at least once according to Hebrews 9:27. The death brought forth the resurrection. In Romans 6:5, the scripture says, *"For if we have been planted together in the likeness of his death, we shall be also in the likeness of his resurrection."* Therefore, each death experience you encounter must be visited by God's resurrecting power!

Today, make up in your mind that to live is Christ and to die is gain. The scripture says in II Corinthians 4:11-12, *"For we which live are always delivered unto death for Jesus' sake, that the life also of Jesus might be made manifest in our mortal flesh. So then death worketh in us, but life in you."* You were born to die and *"Sentenced to Death"*, to gain the inheritance that has been promised by our Lord and experience life and that more abundantly. Every time you encounter a death experience as a believer, Jesus is glorified, because your flesh is put under subjection and your Spirit man is empowered. Our Spirit is the home of God, and we are changed in His image from glory to glory through our death experiences. When we yield ourselves to these experiences, the enemy is reminded of how Jesus gained His authority in the earth, as well as in the heavens and that was because He willed himself to die.

Today, offer up no resistance to the circumstances that may have come to try you as though some strange thing has happened unto you. But according to I Peter 4:12-13, rejoice inasmuch as you are partakers of Christ's sufferings, that, when his glory shall be revealed, you may be glad also with exceeding joy!

Chapter 5: Barren on Purpose

"Barren on Purpose"

In the beginning when God created the heaven and the earth, the scripture says in Genesis 1:2, *"And the earth was without form, and void; and darkness was upon the face of the deep. And the Spirit of God moved upon the face of the waters."* The scripture said that the earth, not the heaven, but the earth was without form. In essence, the earth was desolate, barren, uninhabited and empty.

The definition for the word *barren* is incapable of producing; lacking vegetation; unproductive results or gains; and devoid of something specified; uninhabited. Therefore, there was no life in the earth until the Spirit of God moved upon it. I then began to question God and ask, *"Why would you knowingly allow some thing, some place or some person to be without form, empty and lifeless, when you are God?"* He gently responded and said, *"Daughter because even as you see it in the creation it had to be empty to be filled. It had to be uninhabited so that it could receive its eternal tenant. Like many of my people, it was barren on purpose."* Many of you are saying right now, *"....you mean to tell me that God would allow such a thing?"* Yes, God would allow you to dwell in a barren land so that you could possess a full grown harvest.

The scripture says in Romans 8:28, *"And we know that all things work together for good to them that love God, to them who are the called according to his purpose."* Therefore, if you are reading this and have found yourself barren in any area of your life, God is saying to you today, it was something He allowed to visit your life on purpose. As a matter of fact, it is the barrenness that gives God the eternal opportunity to show Himself mighty in the earth. As well as make you a candidate to receive the miraculous. Hence, if you are experiencing lack of habitation or desolation in any area of your life, rejoice, the miraculous is nigh!

You'll read in a later chapter how I was barren during the earlier years of my marriage. I was unable to produce. However, now that I understand the divine purpose behind the barrenness, I can see what God was after in me. Although I was after a fruitful womb, God was after a fruitful relationship. Therefore, because I acknowledged that I needed Him to produce, He gave me the desires of my heart. God is not a respecter of persons. He wants to give you the desires of your heart too. But you will forever be barren until you acknowledge Him in all of your ways, according to Proverbs 3:5-6. God wanted to find a space to utilize His creativity in my life, even as He did in the beginning. He wanted a visible manifestation of His presence in my life during the time I was barren. He wanted others to know that He was the new tenant in my life, thereby, providing something tangible to show for our relationship.

The scripture says in Genesis 1:12, *"And the earth brought forth grass, and herb yielding seed after his kind, and the tree yielding fruit, whose seed is in itself, after his kind: and God saw that it was good."* The earth went from having nothing, possessing no fruit, to a visible, tangible manifestation of God's glory. **The earth looked like God had visited it.** Your life is getting ready to look like our God visited it!

The scripture says in Exodus 23:26, *"There shall nothing cast their young, nor be barren, in thy land: the number of thy days I will fulfill."* In the New Living translation, the scripture says, *"There will be no miscarriages or infertility among your people, and I will give you long, full lives."* I am impressed to tell you, get ready, because everything about you will start looking like God has come to visit you. There will be no more barren among you. There will be no more desolation around you. There will be no more emptiness around you, God is about to show Himself mighty in your life. His intent was not to leave you barren. His intent was to take you from barrenness to a man or woman of God who has been empowered to teach others how to produce fruit.

In the book of John 15:4, in the New Living translation, the scripture says, *"Remain in me, and I will remain in you. For a branch cannot produce fruit if it is severed from the vine. And you cannot be fruitful apart from me."* Many desire to see a tangible manifestation of what God has promised. However, the key to seeing the fruit is staying connected to its root. You will read in every chapter of this book about the importance of staying connected to the true vine, Jesus Christ.

I know some of you are saying right now, what does she mean by fruit? Fruit is nothing less than a harvest from a seed that has been planted. When you receive a Word from the Lord in any capacity, it is known as a seed. The scripture says in Luke 8:11, *".....The seed is the word of God."* Therefore, fruit is the manifestation of a well-nourished Word from the Lord. Staying connected to God assures the manifestation of what has been written.

The scripture says in Numbers 23:19 that God cannot lie. Secondly, according to John 15:7-8, the scripture says, *"If ye abide in me, and my words abide in you, ye shall ask what ye will, and it shall be done unto you. Herein is my Father glorified, that ye bear much fruit; so shall ye be my disciples."* Lastly, according to Matthew 6:33, the scripture says, *"But seek ye first the kingdom of God, and his righteousness; and all these things shall be added unto you."* **Relationship births results in the kingdom of God.** Therefore, it is no accident that you have gone through a barren state, it was on purpose. God had a plan for your barren state and it was to produce fruit after His kind. In the book of II Peter 1:4, God has given unto us all things that pertain to life and godliness, through the knowledge of Him. As you stay connected to the true vine, He will cause you to multiply in areas of your life where you have long struggled. It is the time for the Kingdom to come on earth as it is in heaven!

In Deuteronomy 7:14, the scripture says, *"Thou shalt be blessed above all people: there shall not be male or female barren among you or your cattle."* For the next 30 days, hear the voice that goes beyond reason speaking to you, everyone that is connected to you will be blessed. I am not just speaking in terms of money, houses and land. I am speaking in terms of fruit that will be added to your account in the Spirit.

In the book of Galatians 5:22-24, the scripture says, *"But the fruit of the Spirit is love, joy, peace, longsuffering, gentleness, goodness, faith, meekness, temperance: against such there is no law.....If we live in the Spirit, let us also walk in the Spirit."* There are nine fruits of the Spirit. These attributes are the tangible manifestation of our transformed life in Christ Jesus. Nine is the number of birthing. It is the number of divine delivery and completeness from the Lord. What am I saying? You have entered into your season of completion and transformation. It is your season of divine delivery.

What has God promised to deliver to you? I don't know what it is. However, you must expect it! Stop being sad and distraught about things you have no control over. Today, you may have awakened lacking joy, peace, longsuffering and all else, but once you read this book, my prayer is that you will walk in joy unspeakable and full of His glory. This year, God will recompense unto you double for every shame. Shame is a type of barrenness. You will see how everything that you have gone through was working together for your good. What you went through last year and this year have joined forces and you will see that all things have been working together only for your good. They are not working against what has been predestined for your life. Every problem, every situation, even those that were self-inflicted have now come together in Christ Jesus to destroy lack and emptiness on all levels.

Barrenness is a type of death. The scripture says in the book of John 12:24, *"......Except a corn of wheat fall into the ground and die, it abideth alone: but if it die, it bringeth forth much fruit."* You had to experience barrenness, which is nothing less than a death of the flesh, to see much fruit. You may still be experiencing shadows of barrenness. However, you must be like David and encourage yourself. Tell yourself that this is that which the prophet spoke of. I am barren on purpose! God's plan in this will be revealed. Therefore, I will be glad right now with exceeding joy, expecting to see fruit any day.

I told you earlier that one of the definitions for *barren* is uninhabited. In the book of Psalms 22:3, the scripture says that God inhabits the praises of His people. I believe that when you and I begin to praise God, we are acknowledging the sacrifice of Christ Jesus. The definition for the word *inhabit* is to live or reside in; to be present in; fill. If you desire to see God move in this place that we call barren, exalt His name, magnify His name, glorify His name, praise His name and He will come in and take up residence in a place that was without form or void. The barren place that He has allowed to be barren on purpose is also the place where the glory of the Lord shall be revealed and all flesh shall see it!

As I close this chapter, the Spirit of the Lord redeemed man from every uninhabited place in the book of Genesis1:2, when He began to move. Today is the beginning of months for you. It is the first day of the best days of your life. God is moving you out and into the wealthy place He has promised. He allowed you to experience barrenness like Sarah, Hannah, and Rachel. Your barrenness may not be related to a child. However, you have experienced a dry place or a dry spot in your life. This is the day that you must sing o' barren, break forth into singing and praising, for the God of El Shaddai shall visit you with more according to Isaiah 54:1. You were barren for a purpose. The purpose was so that God could show Himself mighty, creative and powerful in your life! If you are presently barren in any capacity today, fear not, it's on purpose. Go ahead and praise God – He is bringing you into your expected end. An end that is FULL of results and manifestation.

Chapter 6: The Birthing of Barren Breaking Ministries

"The Birthing of Barren Breaking Ministries"

I remember it like it was yesterday. I thought, "Where did all of this start? What did I do to me? What did I allow to infiltrate my body and leave me in this condition? Why didn't I stop? Was the pleasure worth it now that I am unable to have children? God help me." This was the conversation that broke the pain and silenced an enemy that had been on my tail for 11 years of my life. I had to say it out of my mouth that I allowed this curse to consume my life. I had to say it so that I would first stop blaming God and anyone else for the choices I made. I told you earlier that conceiving anything whether spiritual or natural first begins with a choice. Well so does sin. Here I was paying the wage required for the sin of promiscuity that I willfully committed. Little did I know, the payment would be worth it for the many people, places and things that would be birthed out of me because I chose to endure the process.

From time to time I remember saying to myself, "How in the world can God turn this around? I have made a mess and it appeared to be something that could not be repaired. Based on what the doctors are saying, this could be forever. What will I do?" I believe that in a trial there is always a lesson. The lesson that I learned during this time of interrogation was that I learned how to distinguish the voice of God from the voice of my enemy. I must take the time to expound on this point because until you know the voice of God, you will never be able to conceive and birth out the promises of God. In order to conceive from God, you must first perceive that He is God and know that beside Him, there is no one else able to extract out of you the treasure that is within your earthen vessel.

So many people ask me all over the world, "How can I tell the difference between my own voice, God's voice and the enemy's voice?" Your voice will always speak about where you are. It is the **inferior voice.** An inferior voice is nothing less than a monotone sound. **Monotone** is defined as a succession of sounds or words uttered in a single tone voice; sameness or dull repetition. There are several scripture references in the Bible that will confirm these statements. They are: Exodus 3:11 (Moses), Luke 1:18 (Zecharias) and Luke 1:34 (Mary).

The enemy's voice will always speak to you about where you have been and make you feel unworthy. It is the **inadequate voice.** An inadequate voice produces an undertone sound that is rather subdued. **Undertone** is a low or subdued tone and undercurrent. An unobtrusive or background sound. It is a subdued emotional quality underlying an utterance. The scripture reference is found in Matthew 4:5-6.

Finally, God's voice will always speak to you about where you are going. It is the **overcoming voice.** God's voice produces an overtone sound. **Overtone** is an acoustical frequency that is higher in frequency than the fundamental. There are several scripture references in the Bible that will confirm the overcoming voice of God. They are: Philippians 1:6, Isaiah 46:10-11, I Peter 2:9-10, Deuteronomy 28:13 and Colossians 2:10. Since faith comes by hearing and hearing by the Word of God (Romans 10:17), your faith cannot mature in God until your hearing God by the Word of God has been perfected. In essence, you must read the Word in order to be able to distinguish His voice from others.

I didn't realize that spending time in the presence of God, learning of His Word and hearing His voice would build up a resistance against the word "Not Possible". Before pursuing God in prayer, I was a broken little girl, with no hope. But spending time with God changed me from the inside – out and began the de-layering process required for me and all that would be connected to me, to give birth to the supernatural.

I understood one thing, I was temporarily barren and my heart was touched by women who could not conceive, so that is the field where God placed me in intercession. I began a spiritual campaign in the realm of the Spirit to shut the door to barrenness, that the portal of fruitfulness would be revealed to those married couples who desired it. At the time, I was working for the United States Senate when people started approaching me asking me to pray for their sister, their wife, niece, aunt, or friend because they had been married for a certain number of years and were still unable to conceive a baby. I had so many yellow sticky notes in my chair at work that I almost became frustrated...well I did become frustrated. I thought, "God how can you ask me to do this...I am in pain...we can't have a baby and you want me to pursue you for someone else?" I will expound on another version of this part of the testimony in a later chapter. Both accounts are similar, but when writing them at different times, I realized how Matthew, Mark, and Luke in the Bible had similarities in their accounts in the New Testament of what happened and they also had some differences. All of these books in the Bible were vital to the reader's understanding. So I chose not to remove either version of this part of the testimony, simply for the reader's full understanding.

As I was saying, I had no idea that this level of intercession for others would be the pathway to my success and an intricate part of the birthing process. So I laid aside my personal pain and picked up someone else's. Lord, did I just say a mouthful right there. This is exactly what Jesus did. He laid down His life, so that we might live an abundant life. It is time for you to understand the birthing process of the kingdom of God. It does not and will never include selfishness, but sel**fless**ness.

By 1998, I had a list of 30 women that I would rise early in the morning to pray and serve as their personal intercessor. More than half of them didn't even know me and I didn't know them. However, they were on the heart and mind of God. Thus, I was the vocal conduit that God would use to deliver the promises of God in their life. Did you know that in order for God to exercise His authority in the earth, He needs your voice? The scripture says in Job 22:28, *"Thou shalt also decree a thing, and it shall be established unto thee: and the light shall shine upon thy ways."* Then the scripture says in Isaiah 55:11, *"So shall my word be that goeth forth out of my mouth: it shall not return unto me void, but it shall accomplish that which I please, and it shall prosper in the thing whereto I sent it."* The scripture says in Jeremiah 33:3, *"Call unto me, and I will answer thee, and shew thee great and mighty things, which thou knowest not."* The scripture says in Psalm 103:20, *"Bless the Lord, ye his angels, that excel in strength, that do his commandments, hearkening unto the voice of his word."* Then the scripture says in Psalm 107:2, *"Let the redeemed of the Lord say so, whom he hath redeemed from the hand of the enemy."* **When you open up your mouth as the redeemed of the Lord and say it is so, you grant God a**

heavenly license to intervene in earthly affairs. If you want to see God do the supernatural in the earth, you must open up your mouth and grant Him access to perform His good word that He promised.

As I continued in my efforts to daily intercede for these women, from time to time, I would have a vision of myself seven months pregnant, in a beautiful white gown. The vision was an indication from God that I had tapped into my field of assurance. God was simply revealing to me that the more I pursued Him for others; He would prove that He was not a man that He could lie. He would confirm for me that whatever a man sows in the kingdom of God, that is the very thing that man or woman would reap. Each time the vision would build my faith to go deeper and press in more for these women and surely enough they were each getting pregnant. Some of them were getting pregnant with multiples. They were coming off my list one by one. Not regarding how I felt some days, I realized that I had to carry their babies for them in the realm of the Spirit before I could carry my own in the natural. As painful as that reality was, it was the plan that God would use to get me to my expected end (Jeremiah 29:11).

As I was daily carrying out my assignment in intercession, God began to speak to me and explain that this process in life would not return void, empty or lacking God-ordained results. God was after more than just a faithful intercessor. Little did I know that God was establishing a ministry in me that He would transport to many nations to break the stronghold of barrenness. Like most of us in the Body of Christ, I discovered the birthing process through a personal trial of my own. After many pregnancy tests and multitudes of doctor's appointments, I know by the Spirit that I had made a mark in the realm of the Spirit that could not be erased.

The birthing process that is ordained of God and walked out with God will always BREAK the BARRENNESS that seems impossible. In 1999, we conceived and although the doctor's said I would never make it past three months, it was a sweatless nine months. Not to include only one hour in labor. Barren Breaking Ministries was birthed in 2000, one year after our first daughter, Keturah was born. Keturah's name means "Special Sacrifice". It took both my husband and I to make a special sacrifice in prayer and intercession to birth out that in which men said was impossible. Keturah was Abraham's second wife in the book of Genesis 25:1. God did not stop there and neither did I in interceding for women and others so that barrenness could be destroyed in every area where it had presented itself as a stronghold.

As I continued in my pursuit to set the captives free, in 2006, we conceived again. This time, the enemy was definitely not happy. By the time I reached 16 weeks in the pregnancy, the enemy pulled out the big guns. I went to have a prenatal massage with my sister-in-law, who I affectionately call "Judah" (praise) and my other "sister", Liz, who I affectionately call "Gilead" (heaps of testimony). When I got back home, I expected to feel some soreness from the massage, but by morning the pain was unbearable and I had a 102 degree fever. I had a migraine headache that was causing blurred vision and neck and back pain that I could not explain. My husband took me to the doctor and they admitted me immediately. They began doing every ultrasound they could think of because all of the pain seemed to be in the back of my body and not the front. The baby's heartbeat was normal and activity in the womb was at its normal peak. However, because they saw a blemish of some sort on the ultrasound of the baby, they wanted to perform an amniocentesis to ensure that the baby did not have any birth defects.

An *amniocentesis* is the sampling of amniotic fluid using a hollow needle inserted into the uterus, to screen for developmental abnormalities in a fetus (Wikipedia). Amniocentesis is performed to look for birth defects such as Down Syndrome, which is a chromosomal abnormality. The risk in having an amniocentesis, or medically called "amnio", is that it could cause injury to the baby or mother, infection, and preterm labor or other potential complications that can occur. Doctors say that this is extremely rare. Pastor Derek and I didn't care; the risk was too high and that is not what the Lord told us. When the doctor came in to ask if we wanted to have the "amnio", we both said without hesitation, "NO". The doctor went on to tell us how risky not taking the "amnio" could be for the child and its outcome. Needless to say, we stood firm on what we knew and that is I didn't conceive a deformed seed, therefore, a deformed seed would not come forth out of my loins.

Before I left the hospital, the doctors discovered the problem. A massage of any kind breaks up the toxins in your body and causes those toxins to surface. In my case, what was lying beneath the surface was pneumonia and when it surfaced, it brought with it all of its symptoms: headache, a high fever and body ache. After spending a week in the hospital, my doctor released me to go home and rest for four additional weeks. During those weeks, several tests were done by my doctor and what she saw on another ultrasound of our second baby girl verifiably looked like Down Syndrome. Although, the only thing that could confirm this diagnosis was the "amnio", we refused to take it. Thus, all they could do was go by what they "think" they saw. By the time I reached 36 weeks, my doctor, who is a very good friend of mine, became extremely concerned. The night before my 36 week doctor visit, she had delivered a baby whose parents refused to take an "amnio". The baby was born with Down Syndrome. I was still not moved. I still refused to take the "amnio" and stood on the promises of God. As believers, what you believe will always be tested. The enemy comes in like a flood only to see if the standard of the Word of God will rise up within you. Each time, the doctors came back with a report, the standard of the Word of God that was in me got up. The report of the Lord will always override every diagnosis.

The time had come to deliver. Because of the diagnosis we had received, there were both nurses and doctors on standby expecting the worse. However, Pastor Derek and I were convinced, GOD CAN'T LIE! After continuously decreeing a thing and walking through the halls of the hospital for a while to cause increased dilation, the fullness of time had come. A healthy, beautiful baby girl, Amariah Gabrielle Howard was born at 5:29 p.m. on January 26, 2006, weighing 7 pounds and 4 ounces. Amariah's name means **"God Has Spoken"**. Her name was taken from II Chronicles 19:11. I then realized when I was 12 weeks pregnant why God told us to name her Amariah, because Matthew 4:4 says, *"....It is written, Man shall not live by bread alone, but* *by every word that proceedeth out of the mouth of God."* After giving birth the second time around, I knew that God was the BARREN BREAKER and I was simply His vessel that He would use to manifest it. All praise, honor and glory belong to the Lord Jesus Christ, for the things He has done. I truly believe that had I not gone through a time of barrenness, my pursuit of God for the things of God would have been different. If I had not gone through a time when only God could perform the work in me to produce a child, Barren Breaking Ministries would have never made it to the birth canal. Furthermore, I would not have been asked to pray at the ground breaking ceremony of my doctor's new office, where I serve as her spiritual advisor, when needed. She named the office, Sovereign Women's Healthcare because of her relationship with me. This was one of the same doctors who could not see what Derek and I saw spiritually. Today, she is a very good friend of mine and one of the best OB/GYN doctors in the land. I understood that she was only providing her best medical advice because of the love and care she has for all of her patients. However, God's plan was so perfect and the birthing process would not have been complete without her.

  I truly believe that after I prayed at the ground breaking ceremony, every woman from that point on who enters that doctor's office will be no more barren, but will birth out in the natural which took us 10 years to birth! I am assured that there will be no fertility issues at that doctor's office. God TRANSITIONED the "Barren Breaker" to destroy the spirit of barrenness in their lives both spiritually and naturally even before they ever step their foot on the land. My God is worthy to be praised!

THE SECOND TRIMESTER

Natural Law: In medicine, in the Second Trimester most women feel more energized and begin to put on weight as the symptoms of morning sickness subsides and eventually fades away. Although the fetus begins moving and takes recognizable shape during the 1st Trimester, it is not until the 2nd Trimester that movement of the fetus, often referred to as "quickening" can be felt. The placenta is now fully functioning and the fetus is making insulin and urinating. The teeth are now formed inside the fetus gums and the reproductive organs can be recognized and can distinguish the fetus as male or female. All of this takes place during the 4th – 6th months.

Spiritual Law: It is simply when the Word of God begins to shape you and form you into the image of purpose. The scripture says in Romans 12:1 (Amplified), *"I appeal to you therefore, brethren, and beg of you in view of [all] the mercies of God, to make a decisive dedication of your bodies [presenting all your members and faculties] as a living sacrifice, holy (devoted, consecrated) and well pleasing to God, which is your reasonable (rational, intelligent) service and spiritual worship."* In this trimester, you discover that the seed that has been planted must be fed properly to reach its full potential.

Chapter 7: Fear: Spiritual Birth Control

"Fear – Spiritual Birth Control"

If you ever want to destroy your faith, or the fruit of your labor, you can easily do it by allowing fear and doubt to enter into your mind and govern the outcome of any situation. You have heard it over and over again that Fear is described as **F**alse **E**vidence **A**ppearing **R**eal. Fear is a fertilizer that does the opposite of faith. While faith provides the substance of things hoped for, fear provides the lack of things hoped for. This lack thereof will result in the paralysis of the manifestation in which God promised. Your fear paralyzes your hope. It keeps you stuck in the land of familiar, always wanting to be comfortable, and never inviting a present day challenge. It is the modern day delay or spiritual birth control for the Believer who desires to give birth to the fullness of the promise. I found that it is the one way that the enemy can delay you the longest, outside of committing personal sins.

As Believers, we must allow our faith to destroy every doubt and propel us into the land of promise. I believe that faith is a type of resuscitation device that awakens your inner doubts and places them as a commander in chief of your soul. However, many of us become misguided because although we want the Lord to lead us in all our ways; sometimes that is replaced by fearing the unknown. Although, we believe God; the question is do we trust Him enough to get us to the final destination that He has promised. I learned something many years ago in cosmetology school. If you want to know the heart of the manufacturer of a product; follow his instructions! What am I saying? Jesus is the Elohim God; the Creator of all things. As a matter of fact, without Him nothing would exist (Colossians 1:16-17). Therefore, if He created all things; He knows every intricate detail required and needed to get you to the very thing He created for His glory! But I don't think it is not that we don't believe such a Truth. It is simply because fear keeps us from moving because we can't fully see where we will end up!!

In the book of Hebrews 11:8, the scripture says, *"By faith Abraham, when he was called to go out into a place which he should after receive an inheritance, obeyed;* **and he went out, not knowing whither he went."** It is very difficult to be called out of one place; which you would consider normal. Then to be told of the Lord to move into another place; in which you would consider abnormal. In 2006, that was me! The Lord told me in early June, *"Daughter if you don't make a decision by the end of this year, I will make it for you."* Well when the Lord said that, I knew He was referring to my full-time job. It sounded so strange for God to say to me that He would make the decision for me. However, I knew that He would not violate my conscious. Yet, at the same time He would make His plans known and thrust me into my expected end.

At the end of my own conversation with self, I knew God to be a God of order. Therefore, if this was His intent, He would set things in order with my husband at home first. Okay, I just set some things into perspective for some married women who believe God to release them into their divine destiny. God will set it in order according to the structure of your home. If there is division, the vision that God has given you will be an abomination in His eyes. Because the scripture says in I Corinthians 7:34, *"......but she that is married careth for the things of the world, how she may please her husband."* The scripture also says in Amos 3:3, *"Can two walk together, except they be agreed?"* God's plan is to allow what He has given you to flow freely in the home, without obstruction or injustice to His divine order. Therefore, if your husband is not in agreement with it, you must pray and wait! So, after hearing the Lord say that to me, I didn't say a word. I prayed and waited until He would speak to my husband even as He had spoken to me. Almost 5 months had past, my husband and I had been before the Lord seeking a new way to cancel debt. We were awaiting divine instruction.

On November 3, 2006, I would encounter a conversation

with my husband that would change my life forever. My husband had heard from the Lord. The Lord instructed him to release me into being a full-time wife, mommy and into full-time ministry. Although I had heard this before, the confirmation that the Lord gave to my husband, literally shook everything within me with fear. The Lord told me that I was out of place which was one of the reasons why our finances had been plagued with lack. In God's eyes, I was like the fig tree that Jesus cursed in Mark 11:13-14. I had leaves, but no fruit. Fruit being a sign of the tangible manifestation of me walking in my divine assignment. Therefore, my husband obeyed God and released me into my destiny, giving me all the love, support, comfort and physical assistance that I would need. But that was only the beginning.

Fear immediately kicked in and I was stuck mentally and emotionally trying to figure it all out. I remember crying profusely the day I announced my departure from my job. But I remember the words from a very professional and influential woman in my life by the name of Cathy A. Martin, of whom I nicknamed "Border Buster". She said to me, *"You will be okay, just go around the wall of fear. It is not as difficult as it seems. It is not an obstacle; it is a launching pad!"* Although those words changed my life forever, I found myself with each passing moment, having subconscious conversations about this new ordained move in God. One of the most magnified discussions came from what I could see and now occupationally possessed to literally where I was going and what I could not see. I began thinking, *"What would I tell people? What are people who know that we are already struggling financially say? Lord, give me another month or two. But please not right now!"* I discovered that I would leave a full-time job with benefits, stability, and a direct-deposit every two weeks. This represented what I could see. But thereafter, the Lord would propel me, like Abraham into the very thing that I could not see. This included being a full-time wife, mommy and operating in full-time ministry.

I was paralyzed by fear because I had not done either of these assignments before to the degree that God was calling me to do them. My first month at home was filled with emotional rage, uncertainty and increased fear. I didn't receive any type of severance package or unemployment at my departure. Therefore, I had to trust God or fear what my visual world had allowed the enemy to magnify.

Daily, my idea of where I was going would be so cloudy. But after I pushed myself beyond the wall of fear, I realized that God was adjusting my vision to ensure that I would not miss what He was trying to reveal to me. What am I saying? There are times in your life when you must refuse the spiritual birth control and delay not your harvest any longer. Fear cannot hold you when you make a decision to move. Most of the time we are fearful of stepping away from those things that bring us comfort. However, I am an example of what moving away from what is normal into the abnormal can do. It will cause unprecedented results to be manifested in your life. Results that are far beyond anything you could ask or think.

In the book of Hebrews 11:7, I found such a profound scripture. It really hit home with me and I know it will empower you too. The scripture says, *"By faith Noah, being warned of God of things not seen as yet,* **moved with fear***, prepared an ark to the saving of his house; by the which he condemned the world, and became heir of the righteousness by faith."* Some of you will have to carry out your next assignment like Noah. The scripture said that Noah moved **with** fear. He was afraid of what would happen if he took the next step in God. The scripture said that he moved **with** fear. Which says to me, the fear didn't leave; Noah moved with it. Why? Because he could not allow anything to hinder him from moving **toward** the assignment that he had been given and neither can you. I don't care what it is you are facing, you must move. You must move even if you are afraid to do so. Even if you are not so sure of what the other side will bring, know that God is with you and before you. Therefore, who can be against you?

Let me tell you what is behind you: your yesterday, sickness, debt, doubt, depression, fear and all else that would hinder or paralyze progression. The enemy is trying to stop many of you from moving forward because of the impact it will have on the kingdom of darkness. Therefore, he has launched an all-out attack on your body, your finances, your mind and all else to stop you from moving toward the land of promise. However, you have been given all power and authority by Christ Jesus to move. The scripture says in Acts 17:28, *"For in him we live, and move, and have our being..."* I am instructed to tell you that when the appointed time of opportunity visits you, you cannot stay where you are, you must keep moving. If Abram had not left his land of familiar and decided to go into a place that God wanted to show him, there would be no Isaac. More importantly, there would be no you and I.

The scripture says in Genesis 12:3, *"....in thee shall all families of the earth be blessed."* We are blessed because Abraham decided to move away from his comforts, his culture and his fears to go in a direction where he had no natural compass. Now that is enough to celebrate right there! When you and I move beyond our fears by faith, nations, families and so many others will be impacted. Today is the day for you to move past the fear because there are many that are waiting on you. The kingdom of God moves throughout the earth through the Believer. There are specific people and places that have need of the "kingdom" within you. You must go so that the kingdom of God can be manifested in their lives. I believe that this next move in God for most of us will impact nations.

The enemy could not be this busy for a region or a city. You weigh much more than that in the realm of the Spirit. Remember the scripture said earlier that God has already gone **before** you to subdue nations. This is the reason why you have been under attack. It is simply because of the great impact this next move will bring. Go ahead and take a step of faith. Do it in fear if you have to, but move and leave the past behind you. The glory of the Lord is surely before you!

I began to wonder why it is so difficult for us to move forward by faith in Christ Jesus and why we get stuck in fear of the very thing that is behind us. Then it became very clear. The enemy of the present move of God is the previous move of God. What am I saying? As Believers, we spend so much time trying to compare how God will move in a situation, based on how He moved the last time. Yes, that is a Rhema Word for someone. God is not a redundant God. He is committed to doing new things in your life. The scripture says in Isaiah 43:18-19 in the New Living translation, *"But forget all that—it is nothing compared to what I am going to do. For I am about to do a brand-new thing. See, I have already begun! Do you not see it?"* The things that you have labeled different are the things that God considers a new thing. He has already started it that is why the pain is so intense. You have not had this type of delivery before. It is the new thing that God promised many of you years ago. However, you cannot use a barometer with God. He is limitless and cannot be compared to any one thing or situation.

The scripture says in Haggai 2:3, *"Who is left among you that saw this house in her first glory? and how do you see it now? is it not in your eyes in comparison of it as nothing?"* The scripture in Romans 8:18 says, *"For I reckon that the sufferings of this **present** time are not worthy to be compared with the glory which shall be revealed in us."* There are no comparisons in God. He is always doing something new. What is behind you and I cannot be compared to the glory of the Lord which shall be revealed before us. Therefore, like Jesus, when the enemy of fear comes in like a flood, you must put him where he belongs by saying, **"Get thee behind me Satan."** But you must also remind yourself that II Timothy 1:7 says, *"For God hath not given us the spirit of fear; but of power, and of love, and of a sound mind."* You do not have to fear anything! Because it is clear that it did not come from the Lord.

The scripture says in I John 4:18 in the Message Translation, *"God is love. When we take up permanent residence in a life of love, we live in God and God lives in us. This way, love has the run of the house, becomes at home and mature in us, so that we're free of worry on Judgment Day – our standing in the world is identical with Christ's. There is no room in love for fear. Well-formed love banishes fear. Since fear is crippling, a fearful life – fear of death, fear of judgment – is one not yet fully formed in love."* When the love of God is a permanent resident in your heart; fear has no place to abide. The love of God represents fullness and leaves no room for any other tenant to dwell! Therefore, God does not give you fear or anything that will cause you to delay the birthing process. Yet, he grants unto you power, love and a sound, stable, fixed, settled and established mind. Your responsibility is not to receive anything that would hinder your ability to give birth at God's appointed time.

As I close this chapter, let me give you more revelation regarding how the enemy threatens you or causes you to fear because of the things that are behind you or in your past. The enemy is behind you because Jesus put him there at Calvary. Therefore, he cannot reposition himself. He can't get ahead of you. This is the reason why he tries to suppress you with fear by forcing you to dwell on things in your past. The enemy is empowered only when we give him ammunition. We give the enemy ammunition when we respond in fear to his accusations about our past or about what God promised us and its lack of manifestation. You must make a conscious decision to stop responding to the things in your past. Stop making excuses for not having received the promises of God. God is not slack concerning His promises. He will do all that He has promised the believer, but we must focus on what is before us and not behind us. For this is the day that the Lord has made, rejoice and be glad in it.

The enemy does not have the ability to move forward, that is why he needs your response to act. He needs your response so that he can expound on it and locate you. Your response is like an On-Star system. It provides an exact location to you in the realm of the Spirit. This is why the scripture says in I Peter 5:8, *"Be sober, be vigilant; because your adversary the devil, as a roaring lion, walketh about, seeking whom he may devour."* The enemy is daily seeking responses so that he can devour you. Don't be snared by the words that come out of your mouth. Keep declaring it in faith, not fear, until you see it manifested. Your responsibility is to keep the enemy in his place, behind you. You must KNOW that He cannot touch that which is ahead. But you must do one final thing to ensure the delivery of what God has promised you; forget those things that are behind.

The scripture says in Philippians 3:13-14, *"Brethren, I count not myself to have apprehended: but this one thing I do, forgetting those things which are **behind**, and reaching forth unto those things which are **before**, I press toward the mark for the prize of the high calling of God in Christ Jesus."* You must forget what is behind you and all that is coming against you. You must reach for those things that God has placed before you. But again, this will require a press. The scripture instruct us to press because in order to reach the prize, you must push past every obstacle. This is what I call a press of persistent faith because God is only pleased by your faith, not your fear!

Chapter 8: The Woman, the Seed and the Serpent

"The Woman, the Seed and the Serpent"

I didn't know that the end result of my promiscuity would end up the way it did. I remember thinking, *"Wow, what I thought was fun had birthed dangerous results!"* If you have experienced any type of trauma to your body; whether voluntarily or involuntarily; listen to me very carefully. The enemy is patient; he will await the right time to visit you with the fruit from a sinful seed that was planted. It could have started with a rape, molestation or an entrance from any other type of sexual perversion. However, the enemy does not care how it begins; his ultimate goal is to destroy you in the end. Therefore, he will wait for the right time in your life to cause the fruit from the sinful act to occur. For me, he waited until I was already experiencing a very terrible time in my life to launch his arsenal.

Before I met my husband, I was very promiscuous. I found myself in a relationship that I knew would end horribly. I should have allowed the yellow caution lights to lead me to the stop sign. But no, I wanted to be loved. But my idea of love was always physically based on what I had seen growing up. I should have known when my father hated this guy that I was dating for no reason at all, that something was seriously wrong. I knew the guy was involved with another young lady. Not just any young lady, but a strip dancer. I remember thinking how dumb could I be? But I wasn't dumb, just ignorant of Satan's devices. However, after refusing to walk away, I continued in my promiscuous acts with him. Unfortunately, they led me to a road that I was not prepared for.

I remember being in excruciating pain one day in 1989. I initially thought it was premenstrual cramps. However, there was no other evidence except for pain and a form of clear leakage. I decided to go to the doctor and boy was I in for a treat. The doctor looked at me after running several tests and said, "Honey, you have Chlamydia." I honestly had never heard of such and began asking questions. The doctor explained in terms that I could understand. But the only words that I understood was "severe case of that could possibly lead to sterility." I understood that very well! The last thing you want to tell any woman is that what she has allowed to take place in and with her body has damaged the area that God created for His glory. I was devastated at the very thought of such. The months followed with every three month visits to see if my cervix had opened up to produce a child. But to no avail. I was still sterile.

I began thinking; *"My life is over, no man is going to want me, I can't even have his child to carry his name – Lord what have I done?"* I then made a vow one night to the Lord as I lay in my bed in pain. I remember saying, *"Lord if you heal me and allow me to carry my husband's baby, I will tell other women how you healed me and give them the anecdote you gave me."* Now at this time I wasn't dating and had not met my husband. I spoke what I heard in my Spirit. It is amazing to me that I didn't know the Lord like that yet. However, I could totally relate to Samuel in the book of I Samuel. Samuel continued to hear a voice calling him, so he would answer Eli, thinking it was Eli that had called him. But it wasn't Eli; it was the Lord speaking to Samuel.

The scripture says in I Samuel 3:7, *"Now Samuel did not yet know the Lord, neither was the word of the Lord yet revealed unto him."* I could relate to Samuel. Because I would hear a voice of instruction all the time; yet, I thought it was someone in another room calling me. As a matter of fact, since I was about 12 years old I would have visions and dreams, and hear one particular voice that would instruct me – "I used to say it was my angel of hope." Little did I know it really was "my angel of hope – Jesus Christ, the hope of glory." So after I made that vow unto the Lord, things began happening. I began to see things differently and view men differently. I could see a "snake" coming a mile away. I would be able to identify what was in a man's heart before he exposed it. So I knew that it was no accident, it was the Lord that was leading me somewhere and showing me these things for His purpose. I had to surrender my all to Him. This would be the only way I could walk in healing. It would be to first SURRENDER MY ALL to the Lord.

I did know this much: that "whosoever called upon the name of the Lord would be saved." I knew that I had to be "whosoever" at that very moment to see the fruit of my vow manifested. There was no one there to pray with me, just me and the pain that was birthed out of sin. I just said something to someone right there. When you are going through your worst pain, consider it the best and most opportune time to call upon the name of the Lord. I didn't know what to do next. So I started reading the bible for a couple of months.

I remembered getting saved when I was 12 years old at my aunt's home when she lived in Perry Homes Housing Projects. It was a life changing experience for me. But because I didn't have anyone to cultivate or teach me how to cultivate the seed, it was lost and hidden under the debris of life. Yet, I remember my aunt saying to me one time, *"If you want to see God at His best, find a church where the love of God can transform you!"* I honestly didn't have anyone in my life that was going to a real church. We had our Baptist church that my grandmother and other family members went to, but I wanted something different. I wanted to go to a place where no one knew me and wouldn't judge me.

God's plan for your life is strategic. On Saturday, December 22, 1989, my favorite cousin in the whole world named Mimi was getting married. It wasn't a large wedding. It was just her, the soon to be husband, his mother, father and myself. The ceremony was short, sweet and simple. As a matter of fact, I cried during the whole ceremony. But God revealed to me much later why I was overwhelmed with tears. It had nothing to do with my cousin and her husband. I had found my new church home. My cousin and her new husband did not leave for their honeymoon right away, so they asked if I would go back to the church with them that Sunday morning. I agreed, simply because I knew this was my new place of worship. As I sat in the service, I remember the Bishop mentioning my crying during the entire ceremony the day before. I initially thought, *"Wow, he remembered that out of all the things he could have mentioned."* But as I sat there and listened intently, I knew my life would be changed forever by attending this local fellowship in Atlanta, Georgia.

During offering time, my cousin's husband had mentioned me meeting a young man at the church. Well, I really didn't care to do so because I had made up in my mind that I was going to spend my time focusing on the Lord without any male distractions. However, he introduced me to this nice looking young man by the name of Derek. I said hello, nice to meet you and that was all.

Yet, I leaned over and asked my cousin, *"Who was that?"* She said that they wanted to introduce us last year, but it just didn't work out. I left that service that day excited about what the Lord had confirmed that He would send me to a place filled with love.

The following week would be the New Year's Eve service, so my "Nanny" went with me. As we were sitting in the service, I developed an excruciating migraine. I prayed for the Lord to heal me and sat there thanking Him in advance for doing so. After the service, the nice looking young man whom I had met the Sunday before came over to say hello. As he walked away, my "Nanny" looks at me and says, *"Baby that is going to be your husband."* I replied, *"Nanny, I don't even know that young man. He is not going to be my husband; I have banned ALL male activity."* My "Nanny" looked at me and repeated what she had said before. I left well enough alone, because I would never disrespect my "Nanny". She meant the heavens to me!

The weeks progressed. I was reading and spending as much time with the Lord as possible. One day, my mom summoned me to the telephone to take a call. I asked, *"Who is it?"* She didn't know, but said, *"It's a young man."* I thought, nobody should be calling me, I thought I told every boyfriend and client I had to lose my number. However, I answered in my "I really don't want to talk voice". After a few seconds into the conversation, it became clear that it was the nice looking young man named Derek from the church. He had gotten my phone number from my cousin. He wanted to know if he could take me out for pizza and although I resisted saying yes, I knew for some reason I had to say "yes." After one date, I realized that he was a very well-mannered young man. He didn't try anything or even suggest anything. Boy was he different from all the rest! Yet, I would maintain my thoughts on the Lord. I had gone through too much to allow anyone or anything to sidetrack me.

I began to watch for patterns that led me into sin and would not allow any entrances of familiarity. When you are awaiting the manifestation of the promises of God, you must "guard your gates". "Guarding your gates" include, being watchful over everything that enters your eye-gate, ear-gate, heart-gate and all that flows out of your mouth-gate. As Believers, we must guard everything that God has given us charge over. You are the ruler over your own eyes, ears, heart and mouth. You have the ability to choose life or death in any instance in which there is a subtle entry. Yes, we have men and women who God has called shepherds over our soul. But when you walk in the wisdom of the Lord, you then realize that after Jesus, you are the next shepherd in line to watch over what comes in and what goes out.

This revelation changed my life forever, because I could no

longer blame my past, my mother or father for my own insufficiencies. It all became clear to me. It was my parent's assignment to birth me in the earth, but it was God's assignment to process out of me purpose and destiny to fulfill His plans for my life. Yet, I had to make a choice. My parents had already said "yes" to be God's conduit to get me into the earth. However, once I reached the "age of choice" I was responsible for what I allowed to violate my conscious and hinder my will, no one else.

I figured it out pretty fast, that if I wanted my healing I would have to cease all violating activity in my mind first. I would have to make confessions and declarations that would reflect calling those things that were not as though they were. I could not allow all that I had gone through to paralyze me from pursuing the promise. The metamorphosis had begun and I had gotten too far in the process to go back to my larvae livelihood. I was no more unattractive in my own eyesight. Something in me began to change and I was progressively moving from victim to victor. I didn't realize it then, but I was being conformed into His image. However, it all began with a change of thought. No one else could take the blame for me. **I had to confront some very painful realities about my life and then move.** Yet, the pain was far from over.

After a couple of dates and phone calls, Derek and I

became very good friends and ended up dating exclusively. I realized how much he meant to me when my father died in 1991. He was spiritually supportive, and I had never experienced that before dating anyone. He even provided spiritual insight when some of my family members insisted on me having reincarnated visits from my father as I slept in my bed every night. The Lord sent him at the appointed time to be a blessing in my life. He was not like any one I had ever met before. He didn't violate my space, my body or my trust. He was truly a man after God's own heart. After five years of dating, little did I know that the nice looking young man from the church would ask me to be his wife. Wow, was my "Nanny" right. But she was always right! Oh, how I miss talking to her. She went home to be with the Lord on September 8, 2008. I couldn't believe how God had reserved a space for me in someone's heart, simply because I reserved a space for the Lord God Almighty in my heart.

I began to learn early the principle of sowing and reaping. When I would sow something into the kingdom of God, whether it was through prayer, time or money, based on the laws of the kingdom, I had to reap. I would need this understanding of the law later than in this part of my life. What you learn today is always useful for your experiences tomorrow.

I began thinking after all that I have been through with not being able to have a baby; the Lord loved me enough to send me someone who would love me in spite of my insufficiencies. I thought, "Lord out of all that I can't offer him as a wife, he would walk me down the aisle on December 10, 1994 and commit to an eternal relationship with me. I figured every man wants to be able to name something even as Adam did and Lord you will have to turn this in his favor so that he can give our children his name." The enemy wouldn't be finished because I had my knight and shining armor on my arm. In 1998, our desire to want a child intensified after being married for four years. But little did I know it would be a fight both spiritually and naturally.

I remember it like it was yesterday, when the Lord spoke these words in my spirit, November 1998. He said *"Daughter, the enemy is after the seed; this has nothing to do with you."* This statement made so much sense to me after looking at Revelation, Chapter 12. The scripture says in Revelation 12:1-6, 15-17, *"And there appeared a great wonder; a woman clothed with the sun, and the moon under her feet, and upon her head a crown of twelve stars: And she being with child cried, travailing in birth, and pained to be delivered. And there appeared another wonder in heaven; and behold a great red dragon, having seven heads and ten horns, and seven crowns upon his heads. And his tail drew the third part of the stars of heaven, and did cast them to the earth:*

and the dragon stood before the woman which was ready to be delivered, for to devour her child as soon as it was born. And she brought forth a man child, who was to rule all nations with a rod of iron: and her child was caught up unto God, and to his throne. And the woman fled into the wilderness, where she hath a place prepared of God, that they should feed her there a thousand two hundred and threescore days......And the serpent cast out of his mouth water as a flood after the woman, that he might cause her to be carried away of the flood. And the earth helped the woman, and the earth opened her mouth, and swallowed up the flood which the dragon cast out of his mouth. And the dragon was wroth with the woman, and went to make war with the remnant of her seed, which keep the commandments of God, and have the testimony of Jesus Christ." This woman was being pursued by the enemy because of what she was carrying and what she eventually delivered. As believers, we can learn a very valuable lesson from this chapter. There are times when you are enduring great afflictions, but the attack of the enemy is not against you. It is reserved for the seed that will bruise the head of the enemy. God, now I understand.

Receiving the understanding that the enemy was after the seed, did not alleviate the heaviness I felt in my heart; it was unexplainable. I felt as if no one understood or could relate to my desire. The Lord reminded me of something that I had said for years. I used to say all the time growing up that I would never have children. It was not my desire at that time. I didn't realize how these words would later impact my ability to have children. However, I learned a very valuable lesson. We must be very careful of what we speak, because just like the Lord God Himself will come for our words, so will our enemy. Unfortunately, he used something that I would say out of ignorance as a weapon against me. However, my enemy was patient enough, to wait until the appropriate time when my desires would change based on my sterile circumstances.

You must know that even before salvation, words are a powerful tool. Reflect back for a moment. I don't know about you, but I had some mean things said to me growing up. Although it was innocent on the part of the individual, they were words that would leave a lasting impression in my heart. I had this one family member who used to call me by a nickname. The nickname included the word "fat" because of the width of my hips and the circumference of my buttocks.

As long as I could remember, there were many statements made about that particular area of my body that made me highly uncomfortable and caused me to question my identity. Because most of these statements came from people who loved me, **I knew** they didn't mean it in a harmful way. It was simply their term of endearment or way to verbally express their love for me. However, I grew up with a "fat" conscious and would always wear clothing to cover up my lower extremities. But what I found peculiar through all of this was that the part of my body that I was most concerned about, was also the part that I abused the most. It became vividly clear, my lower extremity was never the problem but how I abused me was really the underlying issue. Therefore, because I felt like I had abused me and had allowed others to abuse me enough, what may have been a very innocent nickname was the seed that I chose to water with fornication.

You must be careful of those things that are hidden in the dark vicissitudes of your heart. The enemy of your soul likes dark places. This is where he hides. If you have an old issue, something that hurt you or disappointed you hidden deep within your heart, something that has not been cut away by the Word, you must shed light on it. Why? The enemy feeds off dark places. There are times when there are things in our hearts that have been hidden for a time. These things hidden could be identified as: betrayal, unforgiveness, disappointments, fear, envy or anything else. When you have not allowed the Word to illuminate that dark place, re-growth could take place.

Let me explain further. When there is something that

happens in your life that the hurt, betrayal, disappointment, or unforgiveness can reconnect to – it will water that spot and there you have life in that dark and painful place all over again. You must ask the Lord to show you those things in your heart that may have not surfaced or may be hidden. Sometimes you are unaware of their presence until someone rejects, hurts, disappoints, or betrays you again. These "emotional scars" can only be exposed by the light of the Word. The Word will cause light to be shed in that dark place. Once that dark place is exposed by the Word of God and acknowledged by you, the Word of God will destroy the works of the enemy and relinquish his foothold in your life.

Whenever there is something that causes some type of agitation in your spirit, ask the Lord to show you its origin. Whatever it is can be used by your enemy to encourage lack of productivity in your life. As a matter of fact, it could be the very hindrance to the desire of your heart. Once you allow the Word of God to illuminate that place, it will set every captive in you free!

As the Lord continued to shed away my personal layers, one morning in prayer the Lord told me to go buy a book. Well, I said, *"Lord there are multitudes of books all across this world. What is the name of the book?"* The Lord spoke clearly and said, *"Supernatural Childbirth. Go to the bookstore and ask them if they have a book entitled Supernatural Childbirth."* So I went to our local Christian book store and looked on the shelf, but didn't see a book with that title. I proceeded to leave and the Spirit of the Lord said *"I told you to ask them if they have a book entitled <u>Supernatural Childbirth.</u> I did not tell you to look on the shelf."* I turned around and went to the customer service desk and asked the gentleman behind the desk if they sold a book entitled <u>Supernatural Childbirth.</u> The gentleman politely responded with a "yes". He further stated that the author's name was Jackie Mize.

First of all, I was a little shocked that they had a book with that title, especially since I had never seen or heard of it except in prayer. Secondly, that God would give me such explicit instructions to get me to the place of my desire. I was so overwhelmed with God's presence and His love as I stood in the bookstore wondering, what my God was going to do next. After the gentleman, looked into his computer to check the availability of the book in the store, he realized that they didn't have any in stock. He would have to order it for me. I placed the order for the book and walked to the front of the store to go out of the exit door and realized I had learned a very valuable lesson from God: **Always follow His instructions verbatim.** There is so much training that needs to take place in the Body of Christ in this area. It is because we hear instruction but when we don't see the resource to get it done, we lay it down and move to the next thing.

We must wait patiently on the Lord in this area of our lives.

I realized something as I was teaching one morning. Both natural and spiritual instructions are divinely connected. I would have a very difficult time in my teen years obeying instructions from my mother. Everything she would say, I would contradict. The Lord began to reveal to me that if we fail to follow natural instructions, it will be very difficult for us to follow spiritual instructions. The two are one! So if you willfully reject hearing and responding appropriately in the natural, you will experience the same problem in the realm of the Spirit when it comes to receiving instruction from the Lord. Therefore, the Lord would have to train you on how to respond, because you rejected the knowledge and instructional patterns He sent in the earth. Wow, I believe someone really needed to hear that!

Your commitment to God begins in the natural. He has given you responsibilities that must be carried out. However, you must yield to those in the earth who would provide directional instructions that will lead you to your intentional place in destiny.

A week had passed and the nice man from the Christian book store called to tell me that my book had arrived. I immediately went to the store to pick it up and couldn't wait to begin reading it. As I lay in the bed that evening, reading the book, I realized that it would be the remedy to every hurt, pain, disappointment and misunderstanding that I had about not being able to conceive. Was I ready for this journey? I was born ready to walk through the valley of the shadow of death. But my God would not let me walk it alone. I was in the company of the great Jehovah-Shammah, the very present help of the Most High God. What I would learn about me, a woman, the seed that I desired and the enemy who desired the seed in the next phase of this journey would leave me full of revelation, power and an innate ability to forcefully take what belonged to me by force!

After reading the book <u>Supernatural Childbirth</u> repetitiously, my Spirit man began to build a hedge around my desire to give birth. I would not entertain any thoughts of pain, delay or miscarriage. I also came to this one very important conclusion: **Because the seed is worth so much and my value is far above rubies, we are both prime targets for evil**. Just like the enemy fights so many believers male and female from connecting with Jesus Christ and excepting Him as Lord. **The enemy also knows that giving birth to another after Christ's own kind would be an additional arsenal against His kingdom**. Therefore, his strategy is to provide a type of birth control in the realm of the Spirit to delay the plan and purpose of God. However, right now the enemy's ultimate goal was to destroy the seed of the woman, so that there will be no traces or evidence of the success birthed out of Christ' death, burial and resurrection.

I remember while working for the U.S. Government, how my life was a prime target for the enemy based on what I had just learned about giving birth supernaturally. Many of my co-workers knew me well. I was precise, had excellent work ethics and could handle any situation. But they also knew that I would pray, no matter what the situation looked like. After I read <u>Supernatural Childbirth,</u> my eyes were enlightened and my Spirit man was ready to fight the good fight of faith. Or was it? As I would daily go to work, I began noticing day to day the challenge that the enemy thought he was setting before me through people. However, looking at it now, it was a divine set up by God.

No one in the office knew the desires of our heart. All they knew was that I was happily married, enjoyed my life and how God had positioned me with what I considered the best job ever. But I began noticing when I would come back from lunch; there would be small yellow sticky notes in my chair. All of these notes were prayer requests. However, as I began to take them to the Lord in prayer, I realized they were not just prayer requests. They were the seed that I would need to sow in the realm of the Spirit to get my own personal results.

All of these requests were requests from women who desired to have a baby. I thought, *"Lord this must be unreal."* Let me say this to those of you who will be transparent. I initially thought after realizing what these prayer requests were, *"Lord how is it that I am even worthy enough to pray for these women and I am in the same situation."* The Lord is ever mindful of where we are; no thing that we experience is a surprise to Him. Therefore, His response forever changed my life. He said, *"Daughter, your release is in your hand! The manifestation of the promise will be birthed as you lay aside your weight and pick up the weight of someone else!"* My role of an intercessor would be birthed out of pain! Little did I know that pain would be my midwife that would birth out of me the very thing that seemed impossible. Yet, the enemy would not let me get through that easily. He would contradict everything I would have read or prayed through conversation.

You need to know that the enemy has no wisdom; he is wicked. The word *wicked* is derived from the word *wicker* like wicker basket. *Wicker* is defined and described as an entanglement or something that is twisted. The enemy will make every attempt to twist, distort or entangle what you hear in prayer, read in the Word, or obtain through a prophecy by his enticing words and fruitless conversation. He will even use people; and most of the time they are unaware and ignorant of the fact that they are being used by the enemy. It was amazing to me how the Lord himself proved this point.

One day at work, our Project Director, who was Jewish, saw my book on my desk. He looked at the book and said something I would never forget. He said, *"Why would you need the supernatural to give birth to a child?"* I began trying to explain; but the Lord stopped me in the middle of my sentence and said, *"Don't try to explain my glory – he will need to know sooner than you think."* Not even 2 months later, he and his wife were trying to conceive and were having serious problems in doing so. He came to my desk one day and said, *"Tapika will you please pray for us, we need supernatural intervention."* The very statement the Lord made to me the months before had become reality. My immediate boss, needed to see the glory of the God revealed in an area where he thought it would be sweat-less! I prayed as I had been asked. Once again, God performed His good word towards them and they conceived and gave birth to a healthy baby girl. To God be all the glory!

I believe that the enemy's greatest form of manipulation with the believer is through conversation. During the time we were trying to conceive, many believers were sent with contradicting conversation because of their traditional beliefs or personal experiences with childbirth. However, because I had built a hedge around my desire, I knew that the weapons formed were arrowless. They couldn't hurt me unless I gave them the power. They were weapons formed against a Word in me that was already prospering. The enemy couldn't win me over with conversations of fear, but it didn't change the fact that I had to fight with every fiber of my being and my faith to win an already defeated enemy. This meant that I had to protect the Word I had received by reinforcing to my Spirit daily, to think on the things that I had learned of Christ about conception. Anything else was a lie and I could not afford to entertain any other truth! I had to allow the Word of God to be the final authority or otherwise the enemy would have won with his deceitful manner of conversation. I then realized that this manipulation in conversation didn't just start with me, it began in the Garden of Eden with Eve.

In the book of Genesis 3:1-5, the scripture says, *"Now the serpent was more subtle than any beast of the field which the Lord God had made. And he said unto the woman, Yea, hath God said, Ye shall not eat of every tree of the garden? And the woman said unto the serpent, We may eat of the fruit of the trees of the garden: But of the fruit of the tree which is in the midst of the garden, God hath said, Ye shall not eat of it, neither shall ye touch it, lest ye die. And the serpent said unto the woman, Ye shall not surely die: For God doth know that in the day ye eat thereof, then your eyes shall be opened, and ye shall be as gods, knowing good and evil."* After reading this verse of scripture I discovered that the enemy knows one thing about women, we like to talk. The enemy immediately appealed to her need to communicate. He enticed her with speech.

The scripture says in John 10:4-5, *"……and the sheep follow him: for they know his voice. And a stranger will they not follow, but will flee from him: for they know not the voice of strangers."* When someone approaches me in the natural, I am always mindful of their conversation. I am very watchful and prayerful. All the while smiling and listening for a familiar voice. It is because I am in constant communion with God, a strangers voice is very easy for me to identify. I began to wonder if the reason why many of us are tricked out of our inheritance through conversation is because we don't know the voice of Christ, or the voice that goes beyond natural reason. I realized one day that even if you can't see but can hear the voice of God, you can always get to your divine destination. You don't need to see in the natural; you need to see in the Spirit. You don't even need to listen in the natural to things that are not of God. This was Satan's open attack on Eve. She responded to what was simply not of God.

It is imperative that you are able to hear in the realm of the Spirit. However, you must be able to know the difference between the multitudes of voices that you hear. We discussed this differentiation in an earlier chapter. The point I am trying to make here is don't allow the enemy's conversation to drive you away from the "Garden" of peace. He is a stranger!

In the natural, every parent I know, including myself, teach their children the significance and importance of not talking to strangers. Well, God the Father is our spiritual parent. Therefore, this same truth applies in the realm of the Spirit. You have been hereby instructed not to talk to strangers. But more importantly, don't allow strangers to talk to you and you respond with nothing less than the Word of God. This statement makes a severe implication. Remember, I mentioned this scripture earlier, that you must be sober and vigilant, because your adversary the devil walks about like a roaring lion, seeking whom he may devour. He wants to devour you through conversation. Silence him with your weapon of warfare. For it is with praise in Psalm 8:2, that we are able to cease the plans of the avenger. Praise is a form of communication. It provides communicated action. The scripture said that it ceases (stops immediately) the plans of the enemy. How powerful a tool is that? When you and I open our mouths unto our God in praise it provides a supernatural stop sign that according to the law, forces the enemy to come to an immediate halt.

I can really see the enemy's attempt with Eve in the garden. He wanted to confuse her spiritual method of communication by appealing to it, so that she would not tap into her weapon of praise. That is a revelation. The enemy is listening so that he can come against the one weapon God gave you to stop him from moving in your direction; praise. You must watch what comes forth out of your mouth because the enemy's ultimate goal is to destroy you, but in the short term he wants to muzzle your praise. You and I must be swift to hear and slow to speak that we may declare the oracles of God and not the oracles of man. If you repeat what the kingdom of God says, the enemy has nothing to work with; neither does he have anything to respond against. The enemy cannot go past the truth that is why he presents a lie. He is lying to get you to give up your rightful inheritance. Don't let him talk you out of your inheritance. Resist him quickly with your praise!

Chapter 9: The Day of Conception

"The Day of Conception"

Before your parents and mine ever came together as one in the natural, your presence was known in the realm of the Spirit. Before the earth or the State you now live in ever acknowledged your existence, you were ordained as a servant unto the nations. Your conception began in the realm of the Spirit. Then you became a living soul in the natural. In the book of Jeremiah 1:5, the scripture says, *"Before I formed thee in the belly I knew thee; and before thou camest forth out of the womb I sanctified thee, and I ordained thee a prophet unto the nations."* You and I were predestined before the worlds were framed for the glory of God. Words framed you and now you exist within the boundaries of that in which has been spoken about your life.

In the book of Hebrews 11:3, the scripture says, *"Through faith we understand that the worlds were framed by the word of God, so that things which are seen were not made of things which do appear."* When you place a picture in a frame, the intent in doing so is to define what is included in the picture and what is excluded out of the picture. Everything inside the frame is included because it is a part of the picture that is most essential to the viewer. Everything on the outside of the borders of the frame has been excluded because it is not a necessary part. Therefore, that part of the picture is shut out. What am I saying? Your world and mine were framed by God. He included everything we need to accomplish and fulfill that which is within the frame (the Word of God). The scripture says, II Peter 1:2-4, *"Grace and peace be multiplied unto you through the knowledge of God, and of Jesus our Lord, According as his divine power hath given unto us all things that pertain unto life and godliness, through the knowledge of him that hath called us to glory and virtue: Whereby are given unto us exceeding great and precious promises: that by these ye might be partakers of the divine nature, having escaped the corruption that is in the world through lust."* You have everything you need to maintain your godly nature and authority in the earth. Everything else is a weapon that will not prosper against the Word of faith in which God has declared and framed for His glory.

    The frame represents the faith required to hold together that in which has been included within. Therefore, the scripture in Hebrews 11:3, tells me that our very existence came together based on faith. You and I were framed by faith! God prophesied our separation, peculiarity, royalty, and our fullness in the kingdom of God before we ever said "yes." This says to me that God spoke the Spirit of man into existence first, acknowledged it and then according to Ezekiel 37:6 (NLT), finished the work. The scripture says, *"I will put flesh and muscles on you and cover you with skin. I will breathe into you and you will come to life. Then you will know that I am the Lord."* He laid the foundation, which is your Spirit man, then gave you a body to cover your Spirit that you might live, walk and do the will of God on earth. Now, that is a God of revelation!

God knew the real you, not the person you see right now on the other side of the mirror. God called your spirit, declared unto it what it would do before the flesh ever had a chance to take control and go in the opposite direction of what was spoken. God took control and framed your spirit man to walk in His will and His way of doing things. He did this before you knew what you would do, who you would become and the reasons why you would resist the declaration of faith spoken before the foundations of the world were created. However, your resistance to the spiritual *"Day of Conception"* was a sure indication that what God spoke and framed on your behalf was sure.

The scriptures says in Romans 4:16, *"Therefore it is of faith, that it might be by grace; to the end the promise might be sure to all the seed; not to that only which is of the law, but to that also which is of the faith of Abraham; who is the father of us all. (**As it is written,** I have made thee a father of many nations,) before him whom he believed, even God, who quickeneth the dead, and calleth those things which be not as though they were."* If you would sit and ponder on this verse of scripture for a brief moment, you will realize that God called you whole, prosperous, blessed and walking in the fullness of His promise; even though He knew the natural fleshly resistance would come.

In Romans 8:28-39, the scripture declares, *"And we know that all things work together for good to them that love God, to them who are the called according to his purpose. For whom he did foreknow, he also did predestinate to be conformed to the image of his Son, that he might be the firstborn among many brethren. Moreover whom he did predestinate, them he also called: and whom he called, them he also justified: and whom he justified, them he also glorified. What shall we say to these things? If God be for us, who can be against us? He that spared not his own Son, but delivered him up for us all, how shall he not with him also freely give us all things? Who shall lay any thing to the charge of God's elect? It is God that justifieth. Who is he that condemneth? It is Christ that died, yea rather, that is risen again, who is even at the right hand of God, who also maketh intercession for us. Who shall separate us from the love of Christ? shall tribulation, or distress, or persecution……..As it is written, For thy sake we are killed all the day long; we are accounted as sheep for the slaughter. Nay, in all these things we are more than conquerors through him that loved us. For I am persuaded, that neither death, nor life, nor angels, nor principalities, nor powers, nor things present, nor things to come, Nor height, nor depth, nor any other creature, shall be able to separate us from the love of God, which is in Christ Jesus our Lord."* God declared through his servant in these verses of scripture, that all things would work together for the good. The spirit man that God called to His fullness in Jeremiah, Chapter 1, shall not be separated from its declaration; no matter how much the flesh wars with the Word that has been prophesied. Neither shall it escape the world in which it has already been framed. However, a true prophecy always comes with natural resistance. It is the opposition that solidifies God's opportunity to be glorified!

As the Lord gave me this chapter for this book, He began to reveal to me the reason why men and women cannot be born homosexuals. In the day of conception, the scripture says in Genesis 1:27-28, *"So God created man in his own image, in the image of God created he him; male and female created he them. And God blessed them, and God said unto them, Be fruitful, and multiply, and replenish the earth, and subdue it: and have dominion over the fish of the sea, and over the fowl of the air, and over every living thing that moveth upon the earth."* God created both male and female and the scripture said that God blessed *them*. God blessed the male and female genders and said for them to **be fruitful, multiply**, replenish, subdue and have dominion in the earth. Each sexual organ of both the male and female has a different function. Each was created to complement the other.

When a married man and woman join together intimately, their individual sexual organs fit like a missing piece to a puzzle. This makes a very direct statement. **Two identical pieces cannot fit!** The word *homosexual* is described as a sexual attraction to persons of the same sex. If each sexual organ in the male and female body has a different function and was created to complement one another; what complement does the same body part have when joined together intimately? **There is no complement only conflict and chaos!**

I must interject something here. In the book of Genesis 38:6-9, the scripture says, *"And Judah took a wife for Er his firstborn, whose name was Tamar. And Er, Judah's firstborn, was wicked in the sight of the Lord; and the Lord slew him. And Judah said unto Onan, Go in unto thy brother's wife, and marry her, and raise up seed to thy brother. And Onan knew that the seed should not be his; and it came to pass, when he went in unto his brother's wife, that he spilled it on the ground, lest that should give seed to his brother. And the thing which he did displeased the Lord: wherefore he slew him also."* Onan used an ineffective contraceptive technique to prevent conception – he spilled his seed on the ground. God never meant for man to spill his seed, but the seed was meant to be planted in **his** wife that the seed could mature, be fruitful, multiply, replenish and subdue the earth. Thus, the seed of man was meant to dominate the earth, not to be spilled on the ground to lie dormant.

When same sex individuals come together in this manner, the spirit of Onan is in full operation again in the earth. Even as God was displeased and slew Onan for wasting his seed, His displeasure continues today and the wages of sin is death. In short, spilling your seed is an insult to the Creator. The scripture says in Acts 17:30, *"And the times of this ignorance God winked at; but now commandeth all men every where to repent."* Selah.

The Lord gave me a revelation that will set the captive free. The image that God created is pure and undefiled. How was that image distorted? Why is it that many believe in a homosexual lifestyle that God considers a misfit? Let me say this before I proceed. God does not hate homosexuals. God despises sin. Sin is defined as a willful or deliberate violation of some religious or moral principle. When there is a connection to anything that will violate God's order it is considered sin. God's order with man and woman is violated when one finds another fit other than the one God ordained.

Before God destroyed Sodom and Gomorrah for their wickedness in Genesis, Chapter 19, Abraham in Genesis, Chapter

18, stood as an intercessor for the people. Although there were many who were entrenched in wickedness and perversion, Abraham's intercession touched the heart of God for the righteous people who were in the land. How coincidental was it that God allowed a man to stand in the gap (Ezekiel 22:30). The Lord knew that man would get in the way of His plan. For this reason, I honestly see why Jesus had to die, was buried and resurrected on the third day.

Jesus told Nicodemus in the book of John, Chapter 3, verse 3, that in order to see the kingdom of God, a man must be born again. Therefore, Jesus had to endure His own birthing process so that He could be born again on the third day. Here are two reasons why Jesus endured his own birthing process: 1) When a man or woman would sin against God to pervert His creation, by attempting to become one with someone of the same sex, Jesus' blood would provide a way of escape. This way of escape could only be provided **if they confessed their sins and faults before God** and turned from their wicked ways (I John 1:8-9). Then 2) Jesus became the greatest intercessor with sin-LESS, uncontaminated blood. He also became the mediator, who would stand in the **gap** for the man, who would disregard Him as the missing rib's replacement. What am I saying? Men who experience an identity crisis and refuse to accept the traits of manhood that God ordained from the beginning do so because they have a void. The void is not because God left an empty space when he removed the rib from Adam to create woman. The void is simply because God's intent was for man to replace that empty space with Christ **in** Him the hope of glory.

Unfortunately, when there is an identity crisis in man, instead of going to the creator, he finds a false replacement – another natural man. God never desired for the empty space in man to be filled with another man but with the Son of the living God, Jesus Christ. The scripture says in Colossians 2:8-10, *"Beware lest any man spoil you through philosophy and vain deceit, after the tradition of men, after the rudiments of the world, and not after Christ. For in him dwelleth all the fulness of the Godhead bodily. And ye are complete in him, which is the head of all principality and power."* When He dwells in man, the fullness of the Godhead dwells in man. Thus, nothing is missing, nothing is broken and nothing is lacking.

After this revelation, it became clear to me how lesbianism was birthed. Women are receivers and men are projectors. A projector is an apparatus used to project or cast an image on a screen (www.dictionary.com). When men in the earth began portraying this homosexual image, women who are receivers were watching and received this ungodly image as a download.

Thereby, receiving the image as a seed that man projected. The result of this image birthed lesbianism. Not to include, the absence of a father and the lack of emotional support and nurturing from a mother causes this seed to mature and develop. This sons and daughters of Zion, is an entrance that must make its exit by full exercise of the infallible truth – the Word of God. The scripture says in John 14:6, *"Jesus saith unto him, I am the way, the truth and the life: no man cometh unto the Father, but by me."* Jesus is the Truth. The Truth must be received and acknowledged as Lord to fill the empty space. However, if not, he or she will continue as a man void of understanding (Proverbs 11:12; Proverbs 12:11 and Proverbs 17:18).

Chapter 10: Until You Perceive You Can't Conceive

"Until you Perceive you can't Conceive"

Every day I am learning something new about this thing called the birthing process. As Believers, we would like to move past conception into the delivery room. However, the birthing process does not start there – it begins with a thought. A thought is a type of conception. It is a seed planted. Not regarding whether it is a good or bad thought, it is a type of conception. I believe that some things in our spiritual walk never reach their level of maturity because although we conceived it, we did not perceive that it was from the Almighty God. Today, hear the voice that goes beyond natural reasoning speaking to you through this book. Our God is well able to bring it to birth!

When a scripture is released into your spirit, it is a type of conception. However, the Lord openly revealed something to me that left me in complete awe. Every natural conception does not result in a full-term baby. Therefore, the same applies in the realm in which we live as believers. In between conception and the birth, there is a very important component - man's will to choose life or death. Dependent upon the man's choice and desire to walk out the conception, his choice will result in its complete or incomplete manifestation. Our God desires for us to be fruitful in every area of our lives. However, there is always a prerequisite to obtaining the promise or the complete manifestation of the scripture, dream, vision or prophecy we received. One of which you just read, is the death of your flesh. But the thought of permanent barrenness is a direct attack from the enemy. Therefore, because the Lord would not have us ignorant of Satan's devices, He began to reveal to me the very process that will deplete his plans and tear down his strategies. God's plan is perfect. It is a plan purposed to bring us into an expected end; an end with manifested results. However, there is a key element that you must be made aware of that will change your very life and allow you to give birth to what God promised every single time. It is simply, how you perceive what you heard.

In the book of II Kings 4:8-17, the scripture says, *"And it fell on a day, that Elisha passed to Shunem, where was a great woman; and she constrained him to eat bread. And so it was, that as oft as he passed by, he turned in thither to eat bread. And she said unto her husband, Behold now, I perceive that this is an holy man of God, which passeth by us continually. Let us make a little chamber, I pray thee on the wall…..And it fell on a day, that he came thither, and he turned into the chamber, and lay there. And he said to Gehazi his servant, Call this Shunamite. And when he had called her, she stood before him……Say now unto her, Behold, thou hast been careful for us with all this care; what is to be done for thee?......And Gehazi answered, Verily she hath no child, and her husband is old. And he said Call her. And when he had called her, she stood in the door. And he said, About this season, according to the time of life, thou shalt embrace a son. And she said, Nay, my lord, thou man of God, do not lie unto thine handmaid. And the woman conceived, and bare a son at that season that Elisha had said unto her, according to the time of life."* The first thing in these verses of scripture that became so clear is that the Shunamite woman *perceived* that Elisha was a holy man of God. She knew that she had an encounter with a holy thing. Mary in the book of Luke, Chapter 1, also had an encounter with a holy thing. When you read both accounts, both women *perceived* something before they *conceived*.

The definition for the word *perceive* is to become aware of; know, recognize, discern and understand. Also it means to identify by means of the senses. When you *perceive* that this Word is truth, then you have *conceived* the truth and at an appointed time in God, you will *give birth* to the truth. There is no thing that you have received as a true conception from God that you will not give birth to if you endure until the end. What is a true conception? A true conception is the result of an intimate relationship with Jesus Christ. In the natural, a marriage is not legal until it has been consummated. The same applies in the realm of the Spirit. Until you consummate, daily commune, spend much time in prayer and reading this Word of truth, you will not be able to conceive. Many women get pregnant by men who aren't their husbands, but what happens after the birth is that the baby has to be legitimized, because the two parents weren't married at the time of the birth. In essence, their time spent together was not legit. It was intimate, but not legitimate in the eyes of the law.

A natural legitimating affords the father the privilege to provide for the child financially, as well as legal visitation rights. God wants to provide for us in the same manner. However, in order to receive a true conception from God, the relationship must be legitimate. God is after legitimate relationships and for those who are not legitimate; we will be able to separate the two by their fruit. A fruitful relationship with Jesus Christ will always result in a fruitful manifestation.

In II Peter 1:8, the scripture says, *"For if these things be in you, and abound, they make you that ye shall neither be barren nor unfruitful in the knowledge of our Lord Jesus Christ."* I believe that men and women of God are perishing because they lack the knowledge necessary to give birth to the ordained fruitfulness of the kingdom. It is simply because they have not **perceived** the truth about their situation. When you become aware of something, it is like an "ah-hah" moment. Then after you are made aware, a conception has taken place because you have received the truth. However, if you don't feed the baby, feed that in which you have **conceived**, it will become malnourished and die. The Word of God is the impregnable truth – it cannot lie. Therefore, there is a missing link to this birthing equation – a believer must maintain the proper diet to see the manifested fruit from the conception.

When you **perceive** that the seed planted is fruitful, then you have **conceived** fruitfulness and at the appointed time in God you will give birth to fruit. It is just that simple! However, something happens in the midst of our journey in Christ that we miss. I believe that there are times in God when He wants to provide a spiritual penetration that will leave us with much or even double fruit. But what happens is that as believers we miss our time of ovulation. Ovulation in the natural is that specific time frame when a woman is most likely to get pregnant when a penetration occurs. There are specific times in God, when our spirit man is ready to receive such a penetration. However, I believe that we miss it because we aren't as sensitive as we need to be in the spirit. How can we change this? This can happen if we allow the Word of God to renew your mind.

The scripture says in Romans 12:2, *"And be not conformed to this world: but be ye transformed by the renewing of your mind, that ye may prove what is that good, and acceptable, and perfect, will of God."* We must constantly allow the Word of God to renew our minds. You cannot carry a baby full-term unless your mind is renewed. A woman has to change her very life to submit to that in which she is carrying. You and I must do the same in the realm of the Spirit. You must change the way you think, change the way you eat, change the very way you live to accommodate the weight, the depth and the height of that in which you have **conceived** from the Lord Most High.

Today, your **perception** must change if you desire a **conception** that will leave you carrying the fullness of what God has promised. There is a transformation that must take place in your mind that you may walk in the liberty where Christ Jesus has already made you free. Begin to seek the Lord daily. Seek His wisdom, His knowledge and His understanding. As you begin to seek Him first and His righteousness all these things, everything that He has purposed for you to give birth to, will be added unto you. I challenge you to try it – it will cause supernatural manifestations to break out in every area of your life.

When you make a decision to stay connected to the true vine in John, Chapter 15, you can ask what you will and it shall be done unto you. But the key is to stay connected to the God who is able to bring to the birth (Isaiah 66:7-9) everything He has promised. However, according to Hosea 9:14, any type of disconnect, could result in a miscarrying womb. Stay connected to the true vine, so that you can bring forth multitudes of branches. It is the way the kingdom of God operates. The birthing process is quite simple. It is a process that every believer must endure to give birth to the promises of God. There is no delivery without a process. Every challenge you have ever endured while on your Christian journey, was all for the mere purpose to get out of you that in which has been invested in you. Today, hear the Lord God today, when you have obtained a true conception from God, your labor will not be in vain!

Chapter 11: "This Looks Like a Job for El Shaddai"

"This Looks Like a Job for El Shaddai"

There is one thing that all of you have in common who are reading this portion of the book and that is all of you need divine intervention from God in some area of your life or another. Derek and I understood that if God did not intervene in our desire to conceive a child in the natural, there would be no other way it could be done. We needed a divine interruption, intervention and invasion by the Almighty God. There are many of you who are faced with "do now" or "die" circumstances. It is at the point that if God does not show Himself quickly that you feel like your life would have reached the level of paralysis that the enemy has long desired. First, I need to say, if that is you and I am moved by the Spirit to believe that is each and every one reading this, then you have been positioned like Abraham for a long awaited visitation from God.

As I was inserting this segment of the book, I could hear many of you saying even as Martha said to Jesus in the book of John 11:21, in the New Living Translation, *"Lord, if only you had been there, my brother would not have died."* Those of you who have been thinking like this, I beg to differ. **If God had come sooner, then you would not be able to experience an undeniable move like the one you are scheduled to experience now.**

Whether you believe it or not, you are right on schedule. It seems as if your situation, like Lazarus', has progressed and appears to be beyond resurrection or resuscitation. However, what God promised you will speak and not lie and live and not die. You are scheduled to experience the resurrection of a lifetime because your light has come (Isaiah 60:1-2)!

Many of you have tried everything to rectify the situation. You have done everything that you thought you were supposed to do. You have even gone to fasting extremes that you have never even tried before, but to no avail. I have an eternal announcement for you: What you have experienced was only so that God could show you a side of Him you have not experienced before. Mary and Martha had not experienced God's resurrection power until Lazarus' death. So for them to believe that Jesus would do something about Lazarus being dead was beyond their understanding because they had not seen God do that yet. They had not experienced that side of God before. Let me say this, just because you haven't seen God do it for you, does not mean it hasn't been done. Furthermore, just because God has not manifested it up to this point does not mean that it is not in the birth canal of the Father for Him to do it. Jesus had not been crucified or resurrected at that time, so Lazarus was actually an act of God to build their faith for the finishing work of Christ.

I had a vision once that literally revolutionized my sight pattern. I saw an opening in the heavens and heard the Spirit of the Lord say, "The cervix of heaven is open. It has fully dilated to 10 centimeters and my people should expect to see what it has been carrying with their name on it and with them in mind."

The scripture the Spirit of the Lord kept showing me was in Isaiah 66:7-9, which says, *"Before she travailed, she brought forth; before her pain came, she was delivered of a man child. Who hath heard such a thing? Shall the earth be made to bring forth in one day? or shall a nation be born at once? for as soon as Zion travailed, she brought forth her children. Shall I bring to the birth, and not cause to bring forth? saith the Lord: shall I cause to bring forth, and shut the womb? saith thy God."* By now, you probably have read this scripture a million times in this book. Get it in your spirit. It will be the scripture that God will use to birth out of you greatness.

The other scripture is Revelation 4:1, and it says, *"After this I looked, and behold, a door was opened in heaven: and the first voice which I heard was as it were of a trumpet talking with me; which said, Come up hither, and I will shew thee things which must be hereafter."* All of this simply means that there is a way that has been made for you that was not there before. **There is breakthrough in the area of your travail.** The travail that seemed like eternity will bring forth a tangible release for you on earth, as it is in heaven. The Spirit of the Lord closed the conversation by saying, "The dilation, the pain, and the obstruction, cannot return void or empty. Something must come from the pain you have experienced and that time is NOW!"

I want to speak to you about one of the many attributes of God, but the one which is most needed in your life right now. It is time for you to receive an increased understanding about the character of God. In doing so, your faith will birth the results of a lifetime. I believe all that you have been through, all that has hindered your path, and all that has brought pain with little to no results will end after you read this chapter. It will end only if you believe in the power of ***El Shaddai***. God desires to show you another side of Him. As a matter of fact, the Spirit of the Lord told me that He was going to show you sides of Him in this season that you have only read about.

At this moment, your assignment is to act as an eternal employer that requires the profession of a side of God who is able to turn your situation before you can say…."Our Father." Therefore, if your eternal requirement for this job includes one who can come on the job and make the crooked places straight and the rough places plain, I have the right person for the job. This person has been in your midst all along. Where you are right now, you need a person who can multi-task and release simultaneously. The need for His presence stirs up the applicants desire to want to apply for the position. I pray you are following me closely by the Spirit. I want you to look at the title of this chapter and begin to write this title every place where you need divine intervention. Your assignment is to apply this title to every area of your life that is unfulfilled and watch God do His best work. I know it has been hard, I know it looks lifeless and beyond resuscitation, but **"This** (whatever your "this" is) *Looks Like a Job for El Shaddai".*

My assignment is to turn your expectation upside down. I want you to assess all that you have gone through over the past year and even months and say it until you believe it, ***"This Looks Like a Job for El Shaddai".*** I know you have heard it over and over again, but by the time you finish reading this you and that situation will never meet again! I believe by the Spirit that your tears and your pain have signed an eternal covenant with the Spirit of El Shaddai. What I love about tears unlike anything else is that when you sow them, you can't reap them. The scripture says in Psalm 126:5, *"They that sow in tears shall reap in joy."* I decree and declare from this day forward that the Spirit of El Shaddai will release unprecedented joy for your unprecedented tears. The joy of the Lord will be your strength. God will restore the joy of your salvation and your days of mourning have officially come to an end. This is the day that the Lord has made. Today make a spiritually conscious decision that your mourning has been turned into dancing. Now praise Him in advance!

There are many ways that God reveals Himself to man. There are also several names by which He does this. The names of God used in the bible are meant to act as a roadmap for learning about the character of God. Since the Bible is God's Word to us, the names He chooses in scripture are meant to reveal to us His true nature and His character. The word *El* is a general term that expresses God's majesty or power. In doing research, I discovered that *El* occurs approximately 238 times in the Old Testament. The word *Elohim* is the first name for God found in the bible and it is used throughout the Old Testament over 2,300 times. *Elohim* comes from the Hebrew root meaning, "strength", "power" and "Creator". *Elohim* whether many have studied this and know it or not, has the unusual characteristic of being plural in form. This means *Elohim* speaks of more than one. *Elohim* represents a unit who has the power, strength and might to create. After completing that study, it all made since. The Godhead is known as the Trinity: the Father, Son and the Holy Ghost, **one God who exists as three distinct Persons. One God who releases out of Himself three different attributes.** An **attribute** is an inherent characteristic of a person or being. So *Elohim* is found in the beginning, in the book Genesis, Chapter 1, when He created the heaven and the earth. God exemplifies His ability to create and reveals Himself through the name, *Elohim*.

El-Shaddai means "God Almighty". In many studies, I discovered that *El Shaddai* is figuratively used 48 times in the Old Testament and 31 times in the book of Job. After conducting many studies on the book of Job and reading all that he had to endure, it is no wonder that he called on *El Shaddai* as many times as he did. ***El*** I found out, points to the power of God Himself. ***Shaddai*** seems to be derived from another word meaning "breast", or "**many**-breasted God", which implies that *Shaddai* signifies one who nourishes, supplies, and satisfies. It is God as ***El*** who helps us, but it is God as ***Shaddai*** who abundantly blesses us with all manner of blessings. As a matter of fact, the scripture says in Ephesians 1:3, *"Blessed be the God and Father of our Lord Jesus Christ, who hath blessed us with all spiritual blessings in heavenly places in Christ: According as he hath chosen us in him before the foundation of the world, that we should be holy and without blame before him in love."* We have been blessed with ALL spiritual blessings and that release would be exemplified through the Spirit of *El Shaddai*. Thank you Jesus for blessing us with everything we need.

I believe that because the Holy Spirit is the manifested

power of God, **all the attributes of God** are performed through and by the Holy Spirit. The Holy Spirit is the **3rd person of the Trinity** and the power cord who executes. *El Shaddai* is the manifested attribute of the Godhead He represents. But that is not all. If you study the attribute of *El Shaddai* you will discover something so profound. *El Shaddai* reserves the right to reverse natural law and to override or accelerate it for His own as He deems necessary. *El Shaddai* has the power to constrain nature, to make it do what is against itself. Let me prove it. The first mention of *El Shaddai* is in the book of Genesis, Chapter 17. God desires for me to show you several scriptures where *El Shaddai* revealed Himself and caused nature to do what was against itself.

Let me first say this before moving forward. Although I know until Abraham's name was changed in the book of Genesis, he was Abram. However, to release this message in simplicity, I will not vacillate between the two names. I will simply refer to him as Abraham throughout. Now, I believe that something happened to Abraham that changed his life forever. This change caused him to become strong and fully persuaded. This new level of persuasion caused him to never waver or stagger again. **Doubt was destroyed because faith was executed.** Most bible scholars have never realized that when we get to the book of Hebrews that Abraham didn't just wake up fully persuaded. There was a side of

God that showed up and birthed a significant change in him and his situation.

As you know, Hagar, Sarah's handmaiden, conceived, brought forth a child, and they named him Ishmael. Abraham loved Ishmael. As a matter of fact, Abraham wanted Ishmael to be the seed that God was talking about. Abraham was 86 years old when Ishmael was born and God didn't speak to him again for 13 years. I have always wondered why God gave Abraham the silent treatment. It was simply because Ishmael was not the will of God. Ishmael was an act of leaning to the arm of the flesh and not the Spirit.

This is a pretty lengthy scripture. However, you need to read it thoroughly to gain understanding. The scripture says in Genesis 17:1-9, 15-21, *"And when Abram was ninety years old and nine, the LORD appeared to Abram, and said unto him,* ***I am the Almighty God****; walk before me, and be thou perfect. And I will make my covenant between me and thee, and will multiply thee exceedingly. And Abram fell on his face: and God talked with him, saying, As for me, behold, my covenant is with thee, and thou shalt be a father of many nations. Neither shall thy name any more be called Abram, but thy name shall be Abraham; for a father of many nations have I made thee. And I will make thee exceeding fruitful, and I will make nations of thee, and kings shall come out* *of thee. And I will establish my covenant between me and thee and thy seed after thee in their generations for an everlasting covenant, to be a God unto thee, and to thy seed after thee. And I will give unto thee, and to thy seed after thee, the land wherein thou art a stranger, all the land of Canaan, for an everlasting possession; and I will be their God. And God said unto Abraham, Thou shalt keep my covenant therefore, thou, and thy seed after thee in their generations......And God said unto Abraham, As for Sarai thy wife, thou shalt not call her name Sarai, but Sarah shall her name be. And I will bless her, and give thee a son also of her: yea, I will bless her, and she shall be a mother of nations; kings of people shall be of her. Then Abraham fell upon his face, and laughed, and said in his heart, Shall a child be born unto him that is an hundred years old? and shall Sarah, that is ninety years old, bear? And Abraham said unto God, O that Ishmael might live before thee! And God said,* **Sarah thy wife shall bear thee a son indeed; and thou shalt call his name Isaac: and I will establish my covenant with him for an everlasting covenant, and with his seed after him.** *And as for Ishmael, I have heard thee: Behold, I have blessed him, and will make him fruitful, and will multiply him exceedingly; twelve princes shall he beget, and I will make him a great nation.* **But my covenant will I establish with Isaac, which Sarah shall bear unto thee at this set time in the next year."** See let me share something with you as it relates to Ishmael. All of this was a surprise to Abraham because normally the first born always received the inheritance.

In some instances, the firstborn would be the one who would receive the double portion. Therefore, Abraham thought that the promise would be fulfilled through Ishmael. God, however, went back to his original promise that Abraham would have a son through his wife, Sarah. As a result, Abraham fell on his face and said to himself in Genesis 17:17, *"Will a child be born to a man one hundred years old? And will Sarah, who is ninety years old, bear a child?"* To God, however, he said in Genesis 17:18, where we just read, *"Oh that Ishmael might live before You!"* Abraham wanted God to fulfill his promise through Ishmael. God could not do this because Ishmael was not the son He had promised to Abraham. Why is all of this so important? What has God promised you? You must know that what you thought was the promise is not.

If you had anything in your possession within the past few months that was not an exact replica of what God promised you, you embraced an Ishmael experience. It was nothing less than an Ishmael birth. It was not the promise. It was not Isaac. There are times when we want God to fulfill His promise through a replacement and God said to Abraham then, and I am saying it by the Spirit to you now - NO, that's not God's best for you, that is not what God promised. Isaac is the promise. You must be willing to wait on Isaac. Waiting will allow you to appreciate the value of the release! Waiting is not a curse. Waiting is the very thing that God will use to enhance your appreciation for what He has promised. The promise is sure to all the seed and you cannot allow waiting to make you halt between two opinions. God's Word and promise is sure and without fail. He is not a man that He should lie.

How am I so sure that you are a prime candidate for a visitation from *El Shaddai*? *El Shaddai* did not show up until Ishmael had become a tangible reality. What point am I making? Your Ishmael manifestation was the prerequisite to your *El Shaddai* visitation. Ishmael's name means "God Hears". This means if you have encountered an Ishmael manifestation, God heard the desires of your heart and *El Shaddai* has come to fulfill and override anything that would get in the way of that fulfillment!

I mentioned to you earlier that *Elohim* is the name used to describe God as the creator, but I want to take the description of *Elohim* a step further to help you understand the dilemma that Abraham found himself in. *Elohim* is the creator of all things. *Elohim* is the creator of the heavens, the universe, planet earth, man and woman. He is also the creator of the male and female reproductive organs. *Elohim* is the one who established all of the natural laws on this planet. *Elohim* is the one who upholds, preserves, and stands by those laws. These are the only descriptions that Abraham knew about God. He only knew God as the creator of all things. So in him and Sarah's mind, they were basically saying, "God, you're saying we're going to have a child of our own, and it's going to be through Sarah.

Elohim has created certain laws that as children we must comply to reach the end of what you promised. One of those laws being that a married man and a woman must have a healthy sperm and an egg that connects to produce a child. Yet, first and foremost, the womb must be alive and not dead to see the tangible manifestation of that intimate connection. This is the law of *Elohim*. God, according to all of this, it is not possible to have a child if the womb is dead. Right?" This is the natural law. I could only create a scenario like that out of my own personal experience.

I want you to notice something. When God appeared to Abraham at 99 years old, He didn't say, *"I am Elohim."* He introduced Himself in a way that Abraham had never known. He said, *"I am El Shaddai."* He wanted Abraham to know that no matter how hopeless the situation may appear, and no matter how impossible it may seem, God is More Than Enough. He is the

Almighty Sufficient God. He will overturn the law so that you can reap what He promised. God's introduction to Abraham as *El Shaddai* revolutionized his thinking and charged His expectation with full persuasion. Hear me clearly by the Spirit, man and woman of God. Get ready because God shall introduce Himself to you in a way you have never known.

Now let me define the difference between *El Shaddai* and *Elohim*. *Elohim* is the One who makes nature, the One who causes it to be; and the One who upholds and preserves natural laws. After using many study resources, *El Shaddai* refers to the One who has the power to constrain nature and natural laws; the ability to override, prolong, reverse or accelerate the laws that *Elohim* created. Let me point out something that I need to clarify so you don't misunderstand me. God is faithful and will never violate spiritual law. *El Shaddai* will however override natural law.

Spiritual laws are eternal and cannot be broken. **Natural laws can be reversed only if necessary for God to fulfill something that He has promised to one of His children.** If it takes the reversing, prolonging, accelerating, or overriding of a natural law to fulfill something God said to you as a covenant person or as a joint-heir, then *El Shaddai* will do it. You need to make an eternal decree right now, and say, *"El Shaddai*, I need you to reverse, prolong, accelerate and override a natural law to fulfill the promise of God for my life!"

The law may be that you have to take chemotherapy for 9 months before your considered healed by the doctors, but this looks like a job for *El Shaddai*. The law may be that every person in your family has not surpassed 3 months in a committed relationship, but this looks like a job for *El Shaddai*. The law may be that based on your credit history there is no way you can get that home, car or bank loan, this looks like a job for *El Shaddai*. No matter what your situation is, if it does not line up with what God promised you, the wind of *El Shaddai* will thrust it into the place of divine purpose.

Many of you know the story how Sarah conceived, and Abraham became known as the father of many nations. I must say this for your edification that names have significant connection in the kingdom. At one point during their process to victory, Abraham laughed at the notion that he and Sarah could have a child in their old age. So when the time came, the Lord instructed them to name their son *Isaac*, which means, "He laughs." Every time they said his name, it would serve as both a spiritual and natural reminder that nothing is impossible with *El Shaddai*.

Like Abraham, I believe that when you get a revelation of *El Shaddai*, you'll never stagger at the promise of God again.

When you get a revelation of El Shaddai, you'll **consider not** what the natural law says or what your circumstances say. You will be fully persuaded. Then the moment the enemy shows up and says, "This will never happen….," you'll just say, "Get out of my way devil. This looks like a job for *El Shaddai*." Maybe the reason you're staggering is because you don't have this revelation. Maybe you're not fully persuaded yet. Then you need to continually eat this revelation about *El Shaddai*. When you get a revelation of *El Shaddai*, suddenly all things are possible to him that believes!

What you will notice and I will move forward is that when God revealed Himself as *El Shaddai* to Abram, His name was changed to Abraham because the attribute that God revealed to Him brought about a shift in his character. Don't you think for one minute God is more concerned about getting you what He promised you, more than He is concerned about allowing certain things to happen in your life that are necessary for character development. Abraham didn't hear God speak to him for 13 years. If that is not a sure space for character development, I don't know what is. Your character is developed as you go through trials and tribulations. Your character and obedience is what produces a pure anointing.

There are many that are used by God, but does their character line up with their confession? Let me show you something about Moses, who experienced a side of God he had not seen before. The scripture says in Exodus 33:17-23, *"And the Lord said unto Moses, I will do this thing also that thou hast spoken: for thou hast found grace in my sight, and I know thee by name. And he said, I beseech thee, shew me thy glory. And he said, I will make all my goodness pass before thee, and I will proclaim the name of the Lord before thee; and will be gracious to whom I will be gracious, and will shew mercy on whom I will shew mercy. And he said, Thou canst not see my face: for there shall no man see me, and live. And the Lord said, Behold, there is a place by me, and thou shalt stand upon a rock: And it shall come to pass, while my glory passeth by, that I will put thee in a clift of the rock, and will cover thee with my hand while I pass by: And I will take away mine hand, and thou shalt see my back parts: but my face shall not be seen."* Moses could not see God's face because God desired to show Moses another side of Him. He told Moses that He could not see His face and live. However, God didn't say He couldn't see His character.

It was more important to God for Moses to understand the inherent characteristics of the God he served more than seeing the God he served. So when Moses said, "God show me your glory", Moses really didn't know what he was asking. God responded to Moses based on what he asked. When Moses said, God show me your glory, He was asking God to **show him an attribute of His deity.** He was asking God to show him His character.

The words *character* and *attribute* are very similar or have like meanings. **Character** is a combination of qualities or features that distinguishes one person, group or thing from another. Moses was saying, "God reveal something to me about you that distinguish you from the rest. Moses already had the burning bush experience, which exposed God's character then. Yet, in the book of Exodus, Chapter 33, He showed Moses His character and what separates Him from the rest. He revealed to Moses in Exodus, Chapter 33 that His character is to protect and hide His beloved from the enemy; not to kill His beloved. This explains why when He passed by Moses in that chapter, He made mention of **the rock that Moses would stand on to experience His many attributes.** The rock was a type of Christ. The scripture says in Matthew 16:18...."....*upon this rock I will build my church; and the gates of hell shall not prevail against it."* Jesus Christ would allow man to experience God in His many personalities without death. Thank you Jesus!

God says to Moses, while my glory or another aspect of my character passes by, I will put you **in** the rock. He said, I will put you in the rock and will cover you with my hand. This would represent the same hand of the only begotten of the Father, the

Son, who would be pierced for you and allow you to possess and experience the release of His many attributes without death. God showed Moses His hand, as a prerequisite to what His hand would do. I believe we should stop right there and praise Him for putting us in the Rock!

I can spiritually imagine how the transaction to release an attribute of the Godhead takes place among the Trinity. Jesus sits at the right hand of the Father interceding for you and I and a request is made known to the Father. Jesus intercedes and tells the Father why the request is legitimate before their eternal court and Jesus say because the request is legitimate and Word bound, "Holy Spirit go and reveal that side of our deity to them. Holy Spirit go and reveal that attribute to them that believe!" Why do you think Jesus left the Holy Spirit in the earth? **The Holy Spirit is a manifested attribute of the one God you serve!** I came to one eternal conclusion: When your physical body and your face is gone your character should remain in the room and still bring about results. That's what Jesus did, He was marred beyond recognition, but left His character and His attribute to exemplify service in the earth and help us move beyond what is natural into what is supernatural.

The scripture says in John 10:9-10, *"I am the door: by me if any man enter in he shall be saved, and shall go in and out, and find pasture. The thief cometh not, but for to steal, and to kill, and to destroy:* **I am come that they might have life, and that they might have it more abundantly.**" Jesus came that you might have life and have it in abundance. God's desire for your life is always for you to obtain more fruit. Jesus was an intricate part of the Father's redemptive plan for mankind. When Jesus shed His blood at Calvary, the shedding of His blood eradicated our insufficiencies with His ALL sufficiency. Therefore, it is time for the Body of Christ to stop questioning their blood-bought sufficiency in God.

The scripture says in II Corinthians 12:9, *"And he said unto me,* **My grace is sufficient for thee**: *for my strength is made perfect in weakness. Most gladly therefore will I rather glory in my infirmities, that the power of Christ may rest upon me."* **You carry a sufficient supply of everything you need to succeed.** When **you** lay hands on the sick, the scripture says in Mark 16:18 that they shall recover. This means that you carry something within you that the kingdom of heaven agrees with – the attribute of Jehovah Rophe, the Lord that healeth thee. Two cannot walk together unless they are in agreement (Amos 3:3). For example, if you need healing, you carry a sufficient supply of Jehovah Rophe to exact vengeance on anything that would obstruct His path.

The scripture says in Colossians 1:26-27, *"Even the mystery which hath been hid from ages and from generations, but now is made manifest to his saints: To whom God would make known what is the riches of the glory of this mystery among the Gentiles; which is Christ in you, the hope of glory."* **It is because Christ is in you, that you too have the power to dispense out of yourself an attribute of God.** How am I so sure? First, you just read that Christ in you is the hope of glory. Then the scripture says in Romans 8:11 in the New International Version, *"And if the Spirit of him who raised Jesus from the dead is living in you,* **he who raised Christ from the dead will also give life to your mortal bodies through his Spirit, who lives in you."** The Holy Spirit will give life to what is lifeless because of the potency of what you are carrying. It is the Spirit that quickeneth because the flesh will profit you nothing (John 6:63). The Holy Spirit is ready to transform Himself into the attribute of God that is needed for your sufficiency. To God be all the Glory!!!

The scripture says in II Peter 1:2-8, *"Grace and peace be multiplied unto you through the knowledge of God, and of Jesus our Lord,* **According as his divine power hath given unto us all things that pertain unto life and godliness***, through the knowledge of him that hath called us to glory and virtue: Whereby are given unto us exceeding great and precious promises: that by these ye might be partakers of the divine nature, having escaped the corruption that is in the world through lust. And beside this,* *giving all diligence, add to your faith virtue; and to virtue knowledge; And to knowledge temperance; and to temperance patience; and to patience godliness; And to godliness brotherly kindness; and to brotherly kindness charity.* ***For if these things be in you, and abound, they make you that ye shall neither be barren nor unfruitful in the knowledge of our Lord Jesus Christ.*** *"* God has given us all things to live a life of exceptional abundance and more than enough. In the eyes of God, you lack nothing and carry a sufficient supply to finish the work and cut it short in righteousness. The scripture says in Psalm 23:1, *"The Lord is my shepherd, I shall not want."* Then the scripture says in Philippians 4:19, *"But my God shall supply all your need according to his riches in glory by Christ Jesus."* If you have made the Lord your shepherd, then you can expect that *El Shaddai* is on assignment to supply ALL your needs!

I want you to see the many times *El Shaddai* manifested Himself throughout the bible. In the book of Luke, Chapter 1, Mary had a supernatural, *El Shaddai* moment that was irrevocable and undeniable, no matter what scientists say. The Holy Spirit impregnated her and caused her to carry the greatest gift ever afforded us, Jesus Christ. *El Shaddai* was the facilitator in this matter, sent by God to override natural laws for a natural woman to conceive and the conception not be by a natural man. God will overturn it for you too!

In the book of Exodus 14:22, you have read one of the greatest moves of God with Moses and the children of Israel when the Red Sea was their obstacle. Per the instructions of God, Moses used what was in his hand, the rod, as an act of obedience unto God. The rod represented the Word of God. Moses put the Word in the obstacle and the Word provoked the wind of *El Shaddai* to cause the sea to stand up like walls on each side of them so that they could go over on dry ground.

In Kenneth Hagin's book entitled, "El Shaddai: The God of More than Enough", he made mention of how the water was said to be "congealed in the heart of the sea" in Exodus 15:8. The word *congealed* means frozen water. His point was not only that the water stood up like walls on each side, but that the reason why the water was able to stand up like a wall was because the water was frozen. No one but *El Shaddai* could do such a thing. Now can you imagine such a thing? You need to be able to see it boldly, because this should not be abnormal to you. This should be your norm. You serve a God who specializes in supernatural performance. Therefore, you should expect this level of spiritual behavior in your day to day activity. You need to say it out of your mouth again, even while you are reading…. "*El Shaddai* do it for me!"

In the book of Joshua, Chapter 10, Joshua made a decree that the sun would stand still. There is no way the sun can stand still and not go down a whole night unless the spirit of *El Shaddai* makes nature do what is against itself. *El Shaddai* caused the sun and the entire universe to stand still a whole day so that Joshua and the children of Israel could get past their enemies. What do you need *El Shaddai* to do for you today? He will do exceeding, abundantly, above anything you ask or think! You need to say out of your mouth, "*El Shaddai* do it for me!" In the book of Joshua, Chapter 6, many of you have read about the Jericho walls and how they collapsed. Jericho was a walled city and presented major obstacles for the Hebrews because it was right in the middle of their path into the Promised Land. So the Jericho wall had to go because it was in the direct pathway of their land of victory! However, let me shed some light on something. You know the story, for six days the army would circle the city once while the priests blew their ram's horns. The priests with trumpets went first, then the priests which carried the Ark of the Covenant, then the army. The only sound that would be heard would be the sound of the horns; no one could speak a word. Some of us would not have made it! Then on the seventh day, they would circle the city seven times in the same manner. When Joshua gave the signal, they would shout with a great shout. The walls would fall flat and they would run into the city. The scripture says in Joshua 6:15-21, *"Early on the seventh day, they started at dawn and marched around the city seven times in the same way. That was the only day they marched around the city seven times. After the seventh time, the priests blew the trumpets, and Joshua said to the people, "Shout! For the LORD has given you the city.* **But the city and everything in it are set apart to the LORD for destruction**. *Only Rahab the prostitute and everyone with her in the house will live, because she hid the men we sent.* [18] *But keep yourselves from the things set apart, or you will be set apart for destruction. If you take any of those things, you will set apart the camp of Israel for destruction and bring disaster on it. For all the silver and gold, and the articles of bronze and iron, are dedicated to the LORD and must go into the LORD's treasury. So the people shouted, and the trumpets sounded. When they heard the blast of the trumpet, the people gave a great shout, and the wall collapsed. The people advanced into the city, each man straight ahead, and they captured the city. They completely destroyed everything in the city with the sword—every man and woman, both young and old, and every ox, sheep, and donkey."* Joshua told them, and I will paraphrase: "…do exactly what God said, but don't you take anything out of this place. Everything has been set apart for God's destruction. The walls will come down, but the stuff that is in this city belongs to God....don't touch it or you will suffer destruction." What happened thereafter baffled me because the walls fell down flat.

One description said that the walls fell down through the ground. Another description said that the walls fell so strategically that they created a ramp for them to walk straight into the city. Either way, they were able to walk straight into a place where there was no going in and no going out. NO BODY COULD DO THAT BUT EL SHADDAI!!! *El Shaddai* will cause a sudden manifestation of the new thing that God promised and tear down the old thing once and for all!! You need to say it until you mean it, *El Shaddai,* DO IT FOR ME! Let the walls fall flat down so that I can go in without obstruction! I have always wondered how Jesus fed 5,000 people with two fish and five loaves of bread in the book of Matthew 14:15-21. IT IS NOT HUMANLY POSSIBLE! But according to Philippians 4:19, *El Shaddai* is the great supplier and Jesus extracted an attribute out of Himself and God the Father released it! If you don't hear anything else, hear me say this: IT IS TIME FOR YOU TO EXTRACT OUT OF YOURSELF AN ATTRIBUTE OF GOD THAT WILL BRING VICTORY IN EVERY AREA OF YOUR LIFE! It is the attribute of *El Shaddai*. Jesus was able to distribute more than enough because He is the Great Distributor. I know I have said it before in this message, but it is worth repeating again. God will always perform exceeding, abundantly, above anything we can ask or think. Why am I telling you all of this? This is the God that you serve. He is *El Shaddai.* He is not a respecter of persons. If He did it for them, all you have to do is believe that He will do it for you. You are already a candidate because you have ran out of "You" options! In the book of Daniel, Chapter 3, we know the three Hebrew boys: Shadrach, Meschach and Abednego who refused to bow down and worship the graven image. Therefore, the king threw them in a fire that was 7 times hotter than normal. According to the laws of nature if anything is placed in a fire it is supposed to burn beyond recognition. However, that is not so when *El Shaddai* is on the scene. The 4th man in the fire was none other than the Spirit of *El Shaddai*!!! He was in the fire with the three Hebrew boys causing the fire to do what was against itself! I can see the Holy Spirit blowing the flames so that no plague would come near the three Hebrew boys dwelling. What force of nature do you need *El Shaddai* to constrain to get you what has been promised you? Whatever it is, *El Shaddai* will make it turn in your favor! In Luke, Chapter 5, the disciples had been toiling all night long and had caught nothing and were washing their nets because they had literally given up. Then Jesus shows up and gives them shifting instructions. This word is filled with shifting instructions for you. Do not miss your moment! So Jesus tells them to pick back up your net and go deeper! I don't know who this portion of the book was written for, but you must launch out into the deep to get this manifestation because you cannot experience it near the shallow waters! You cannot be halting between two opinions if you want this level of visitation. You must be fully persuaded and doubt not in your heart! When the disciples dropped their nets, it was as if they dropped the place that they looked to for their security. When they did this they were able to pick up the abundant supply that the spirit of *El Shaddai* brings. Do you remember the story in John, Chapter 2, verse 1 where Jesus turned the water into wine? This was the first miracle He performed. Do you realize how long it takes from the time you plant the seed to produce the vine that produces the grapes that become the wine? In the natural, it takes two to three years. Wine alone takes two to three years to mature, but the best wine takes anywhere from five to six years.

The scripture says in John 2:9-10, *"When the ruler of the feast had tasted the water that was made wine, and knew not whence it was: but the servants which drew the water... And saith unto him, Every man at the beginning doth set forth good wine; and when men have well drunk, then that which is worse: but thou hast kept the good wine until now." El Shaddai* accelerated a law that normally takes six years to mature in a split second. Based on this information, you should not still be trying to figure out how is

God going to provide the finances to pay your light bill? "Time's running out. God, if you don't intervene, it's going to be cut off." Go ahead and praise Him in advance because "This Looks like a job for *El Shaddai*." If you're under pressure and in the natural it seems impossible, then it's time for you to get a revelation of *El Shaddai* and walk in it.

In the book of John 8:7-8, you find the Pharisees who bring a woman to Jesus who is caught in adultery. They said that the law of Moses command that this woman should be stoned. While they are speaking, Jesus stoops down and with His finger wrote on the ground as if He didn't hear them. So they continued asking Him and Jesus finally replies in John 8:7-8. The scripture says, *"....He that is without sin among you, let him first cast a stone at her. And again he stooped down, and wrote on the ground."* The law according to Deuteronomy 9:10 and Exodus 31:18 was written with the finger of God.

When Jesus stooped down to write on the ground He was saying without saying it: **I wrote the law, therefore, I can reverse it.** Woman where are your accusers? What point am I making? I see God writing on the ground on your behalf. Many of you have been accused but your God wrote the law, therefore, He can reverse it. Look for God to reverse that which seems irreversible. God has stooped down on the ground today and wrote a new law for you that would represent His kingdom. Therefore, the earth must respond with the harvest that your faithful seeds have provoked. Praise Him, for your eyes have not seen. This Word from the Almighty God will provoke manifestation and it shall not be by might, nor by power, but by His Spirit.

Chapter 12: "Whose Seed Is In Itself"

"Whose Seed is in Itself"

As members of the commonwealth society of the kingdom of God, you are carrying the most precious eternal cargo on the inside of you that has ever been given to man. However, because you are the carrier and the conduit, you must be careful not to carry any other weight that would hinder productivity. The scripture says in Amos 3:3, *"Can two walk together, except they be agreed?"* I have learned that if it is not in alignment or agreement with the Word of God, it is impossible for me to digest it properly because I am a spiritual carnivore (meat-eater) of His Holy Word. Thus, I maintain my distance from anything that has the ability to contaminate the seed of Christ on the inside of me. There are even people of which I will never connect with because while they are not unsaved, I have discerned that being around them could cause spiritual indigestion. So I remain spiritually aware of what I allow to come near the seed on the inside of me that will produce after its own kind again and again.

The scripture says in Genesis 8:22, *"While the earth remaineth, seedtime and harvest, and cold and heat and summer and winter, and day and night shall not cease."* This scripture is saying something to the sower that I am just seeing clearly. It basically says that as long as the earth remains in existence, in

EVERY SEASON, whether it is cold, heat, summer, winter, day or night there will always be seedtime and harvest. This means, you don't have to expect to only reap in one season, you should expect to reap in every season. Because in every season, there will be SEEDTIME AND HARVEST. All praise, honor and glory belong to the Spirit of the Living God who is a God of great revelation.

I must interject something here that I believe is divinely connected to the direction in which the Spirit of the Lord desires for me to take in this chapter. Four weeks before this book went to print, God was doing a work in me that until now, I wasn't able to fully explain. In February, 2012, I realized after preaching in New Jersey, then leaving there and weeks later preaching in Pensacola, Florida that while God had the anointing on my life on an assignment to remove burdens and destroy yokes in the lives of others, the same would not return void in my own life. God would not allow the burdens in my life to remain, but as I was moving in Him, one by one, the burdens were removed and the yoke was destroyed. As I was collapsing the time zones in the realm of the Spirit for others, God in His sovereignty was redeeming the time for me. As I was declaring rest for others, I had entered into the rest of God for myself. There was full persuasion, without the manifestation, but with divine assurance in me and all around me. Before realizing it, I knew what it really meant **to take His yoke**

upon me. For His yoke was without a doubt, easy and His burden, light.

The scripture says in the book of Matthew 11:28-30, *"Come unto me, all ye that labour and are heavy laden, and I will give you rest. Take my yoke upon you, and learn of me; for I a meek and lowly in heart: and ye shall find rest unto your souls. For my yoke is easy, and my burden is light."* First of all, let me tell you what I discovered. The definition of a *yoke* according to Webster's dictionary is a wooden crosspiece that is fastened over the necks of two animals and attached to the plow or cart that they are to pull. As I read this definition, I have never had such a clear visual of something in my life.

It was never God's intent for you to pull the many "carts" in your life. Those "carts" are the result of your feeling as if you are not moving in the direction that God promised. So you pick up things that are not relevant to where God is taking you and they become a weight. In essence, it is a yoke that didn't come from God. The scripture says in the book of Galatians 5:7-8, *"Ye did run well; who did hinder you that ye should not obey the truth?* ***This persuasion cometh not of him that calleth you.****"* If the "carts" or cares of this world can hinder your ability from moving forward, then you have been persuaded in a manner that didn't come from God and an exchange must be made. You must take

His yoke upon you. Being in ministry you get to see many delivered, and many that obtain their release from what the Spirit of the Lord instructed you to minister to them. However, when the individual you prophesied to obtains the tangible manifestation of what the Spirit of the Lord instructed you to speak, that is your evidence that surely God had to hear your own requests. Thus, God will not cause you to conceive in His presence and not bring to birth (Isaiah 66:7-9). Someone needed to hear this so that you will know, God has not forgotten you. He will bring to pass what has been decreed, what has been prophesied and what has been spoken. As a matter of truth, you are carrying the seed that possesses the power in itself to bring to pass that which is not seen. Do not be deceived, the seed you planted was not insignificant. It was packed with fullness.

Since 2000, the Lord has allowed me to write a Word for the Week and a Seed of Empowerment for all to read and be encouraged. Today, the words, **Seed of Empowerment** took on another meaning. In Romans 4:16, the scripture says, *"Therefore, it is of faith, that it might be by grace; to the end **the promise might be sure to all the seed**; not to that only which is of the faith of Abraham; who is the father of us all."* There is one thing that I have recognized about a **seed** that God planted and that is **it is EMPOWERED to produce after its kind.**

The scripture says in Genesis 1:11-12, *"And God said, Let the earth bring forth grass, the herb yielding seed, and the fruit tree yielding fruit after his kind, whose seed is in itself, upon the earth: and it was so. And the earth brought forth grass, and herb yielding seed after his kind, and the tree yielding fruit, whose seed was in itself, after his kind: and God saw that it was good."* The **seed** may look insignificant, **but the release or the promise that will spring from it is sure, potent and powerful.** In this verse of scripture in the book of Genesis, I discovered a spiritual nugget that will last eternally. The scripture above stated TWICE, *"....whose seed is in itself."* I immediately became aware in my spirit man that God was saying something to us that many of us probably have missed for years. God in His great wisdom, created these plants with the seed already in them to bring forth more of their kind. What point am I making? **God created you and I with the seed already in us to bring forth more of His kind in the earth.**

As joint-heirs with Christ, we are not deficient in any area of our lives, because His grace is sufficient (II Corinthians 12:9-10) towards us. Christ in you, the hope of glory is the mystery that has been hidden from ages and generations, but now is made manifest to His saints. What started out as the Word became flesh and now dwells not just among you, but IN YOU! I don't know what the enemy has told you lately, **but what started out as a Word from God, shall NOW be made flesh and dwell among you.** You can apply this to every area of your life where you got a Word from God. The end result is that it will come to pass and become tangible and physical in this earthly realm. It cannot remain a seed. IT MUST PRODUCE AND ACCOMPLISH what it was released to accomplish. IT WAS RELEASED TO BECOME A HARVEST, NOT TO REMAIN A SEED!

The scripture says in Luke 8:11, *"Now the parable is this: the seed is the word of God."* Jesus is speaking in this verse of scripture and He says that the **seed** is the **Word of God**. Therefore, we must come to two eternal conclusions: 1) The scripture says in Isaiah 55:10-11 in the Message Translation, *"Just as rain and snow descend from the skies and don't go back until they have watered the earth, Doing their work of making things grow and blossom, producing seed for farmers and food for the hungry, So will the words that come out of my mouth not come back empty handed. They'll do the work I sent them to do, they'll complete the assignment I gave them."* First, we know that when the Word of God is released, it cannot come back void, empty or lacking results. **It must be returned as produce (fruit) and not a seed.** This is a good time to shout and tell the devil, "You had part of it right. I will never see what I decreed. But what you didn't say is that I will never see it as a seed, but NOW IS COME the time that I will see it as manifested fruit, in Jesus name." 2) The scripture says in John 1:1-3, 14, *"In the beginning was the Word, and the Word was with God, and the Word was God. The same was in the beginning with God. All things were made by him; and without him was not any thing made that was made ....And the Word was made flesh, and dwelt among us, (and we beheld his glory, the glory as of the only begotten of the Father,) full of grace and truth."* Since the seed is the Word of God, it cannot remain a seed. It must be made flesh and a tangible reality and dwell in the midst of its recipient.

This **Seed** of Empowerment, this word of encouragement that the Spirit of the Lord instructed me to release in this chapter will not return unto you void of manifestation. It will produce after God's own kind. Why? The fullness of the Godhead dwells within you bodily and there is no seed planted by God that can return void of His visitation or manifestation.

For the past couple of weeks, I have had an overwhelming anticipation in my Spirit man. The kind of anticipation that awakes you at least two or three times throughout the night, looking and waiting for something to appear. The getting up throughout the night was a sure sign that something else was about to be birthed. I know, not I heard, but I know that with everything that is operating in me by the Holy Ghost that the Body of Christ is on the verge of receiving the tangible manifestation of all things – I know this! I believe your season has changed. **I know by the Spirit that there will be no more schism between what God said and what you see.** The two shall become one and dwell among you.

Hear me clearly by the Spirit when I say to you that according to the book of Matthew 6:10, *"Thy kingdom come. Thy will be done in earth, as it is in heaven."* Many of you have fasted, died to your flesh, prayed, waited and died to your flesh again. I believe that waiting in this season will allow you to appreciate the value of this supernatural release. I further believe that you need not become complacent and comfortable where you are because **it is time to give birth again. But this time when you birth it, it will not be as in times past.**

The scripture says in II Samuel 7:10-11, 25-26, *"Moreover I will appoint a place for my people Israel, and will plant them, that they may dwell in a place of their own, and move no more;* **neither shall the children of wickedness afflict them any more, as beforetime**, *And as since the time that I commanded judges to be over my people Israel, and have caused thee to rest from all thine enemies. Also the Lord telleth thee that he will make thee an house...And now, O Lord God, the word that thou hast spoken* *concerning thy servant, and concerning his house,* **establish it** *for ever, and do as thou hast said. And let thy name be magnified for ever, saying, The Lord of hosts is the God over Israel: and let the house of thy servant David be established before thee."* God will do what He said in this season. **Affliction shall not arise a second time (Nahum 1:9) or like beforetime** as the scripture has said. He will give you rest from your enemies and as promised He will plant you, which means to ESTABLISH you and cause you to birth the impossible.

You will never again be uprooted out of a land that rightfully belongs to you. God has purposed in this season **to permanently position you** in the land of peace, joy, victory, healing, abundance and liberty. **This time will not be like the times before. This time will not be like the times before. This time will not be like the times before. This time will not be like the times before. This is not a typographical error. Faith comes by hearing and hearing by the Word of God. Hear it by the Spirit: THIS TIME WILL NOT BE LIKE THE TIMES BEFORE.** You can yield to this season of liberty. You can yield to this season of delivery. You can let your guard down. You will not be hurt or disappointed like in times past. This is a new season and a new day. A fresh anointing is coming your way. It's the season of power and prosperity. Believe the prophets of the Lord when they say that it is a new season and IT IS COME to you today (II Chronicles 20:20). How am I so sure? God cannot lie and there have not, neither will there ever be ONE WORD that has failed of which He has promised (I Kings 8:56). Men have failed you, but God cannot and will never fail you. There is no variableness or inconsistency in Him (James 1:17).

The scripture says in Deuteronomy 11:10-12, 14-15, *"For the land, whither thou goest to possess it, is not as the land of Egypt, from whence ye came out, where thou sowedest thy seed, and wateredst it with thy foot, as a garden of herbs: But the land, whither ye go to possess it, is a land of hills and valleys, and drinketh water of the rain of heaven: A land which the Lord thy God careth for: the eyes of the Lord thy God are always upon it, from the beginning of the year even unto the end of the year.....That I will give you the rain of your land in his due season, the first rain and the latter rain, that thou mayest gather in thy corn, and thy wine, and thine oil. And I will send grass in thy fields for thy cattle, that though mayest eat and be full."* God has been watching over the Word spoken over your life to perform it. In this season of performance, you will not sow a seed and not reap the benefits. There will be a quick return on your investment in this season. Even as God will receive a return on His investment of the seed He placed in you. It sounds as if this is spiritual Wall

Street and the Dow Jones is at its peak and the stock market is on the rise. Something glorious is scheduled to come out of the seed that was imparted into you. IT IS CALLED MANIFESTATION!

The end has come to some things and a new beginning has sprung forth for other things. It is a time in God for you to DO IT AGAIN! It is a time in God for you to START OVER! It is a time in God to regain your spiritual awareness and move forward in victory to the choreographic movements of the kingdom. It is time for you to have and to hold from this day forward. Again, it's a new season and it's a new day. As a matter of fact, despite what you see, it is a season of victory on the right hand and on the left. On every side shall be a blessing.

The scripture says in Ezekiel 34:26-28, *"And I will make them and the places round about my hill a blessing; and I will cause the shower to come down in his season; there shall be showers of blessing.* **And the tree of the field shall yield her fruit,** *and the earth shall yield her increase, and they shall be safe in their land,* **and shall know that I am the Lord, when I have broken the bands of their yoke,** *and delivered them out of the hand of those that served themselves of them. And they shall no more be a prey to the heathen, neither shall the beast of the land devour them; but they shall dwell safely, and none shall make them afraid."* Selah.

There is so much more coming than what you have seen in God in times past. I was sitting on my bed and kept hearing the Holy Spirit sing the words to a song by Mary Alesse. The lyrics to the song say, *"More, we ask for more, more of your power, and more of your glory. More, we ask for more, more of your Spirit and more of your presence, like we've never known before. All we ask you Lord, is for more....More of you, nothing less will do, Lord we ask of you, give us more."* To whom much is given in this season, much more will be required. Therefore, **the more you partake of the Word of God, the more birthing God will require of you.** Each scripture serves as a seed and a conception that will result in a divine delivery. **In this season, you will not be able to read, study or commune with God and not birth out the results of what you ate.** Again, the two will walk together in agreement.

The scripture says in John 3:6, *"That which is born of the flesh is flesh; and that which is born of the Spirit is spirit."* As a matter of fact, I will go back to Genesis 8:22 because as long as the earth remains every seed that has been planted in you through and by the semen of the Father will bring about produce (fruit). Therefore, put your feet back in the eternal stirrups and be prepared to push again. **You cannot leave bearing** and you cannot stop birthing until you have given birth to Judah.

In the book of Genesis, Chapter 29, you find Leah who had given birth to three other children before Judah. The scripture says in Genesis 29:31-35, *"And when the Lord saw that Leah was hated, he opened her womb: but Rachel was barren. And Leah conceived, and bare a son, and she called his name Reuben: for she said, Surely the Lord hath looked upon my affliction; now therefore my husband will love me. And she conceived again and bare a son; and said, Because the Lord hath heard that I was hated, he hath therefore given me this son also: and she called his name Simeon. And she conceived again, and bare a son; and said, Now this time will my husband be joined to me, because I have born him three sons: therefore was his name called Levi. And she conceived again, and bare a son: and she said, Now will I praise the Lord: therefore she called his name Judah; and left bearing."* The firstborn was Reuben, his name meant "behold a son"; the second son's name was Simeon, his name meant "he has heard"; the third son's name was Levi, his name meant, "joining or to join". The Levitical tribe was birthed out of this 3rd son. Yet, when Leah gave birth to the fourth son, Judah, she gave him that name because the manifestation of this final birth or push was not connected to her relationship with her husband but was connected to her relationship with the Almighty God.

What point am I making? **The manifestation of this next**

push in your life will not be connected to those you know in the natural, but it will be connected to the God who will continue to produce in you after His kind because of the relationship you have with Him. You have given birth to many things, but this next birth will mean something more to God than any of the other births. Hold on, I must stop and PRAISE Him right here. HALLELUJAHHH! Thank you Jesus! Now I know based on this that it will all be worth the sacrifice. (Thank you Prophetess Amichia Jones for confirmation.)

Now let me finish where I left off. "Judah" means praise. Praise ceases the plans of the avenger (Psalm 8:2). Leah would not stop until she had given birth to that which would place a cease and desist order on her enemy. Here is the reason why you cannot stop until you give birth to Judah, because the scripture says in Psalm 60:7 that Judah is the lawgiver. **Judah sets the law and establishes boundaries for the rest.** This next birth will establish, set the law and establish boundaries for whatever else you will birth in God. Thus, the gates of hell cannot prevail against it.

Leah had something that I never noticed. **She would not stop until she had reached the birth that would glorify God and not man.** Each time she conceived, **each time a seed was planted** and the birth did not turn out in the manner in which she desired, **it built her confidence to do it again.** I want you to hear me today by the Spirit. Each time you received the semen of His Word and birthed out the manifestation of what you received, **you must conceive again until God is finished using you as a conduit to birth greatness in the earth!**

Each birth for Leah was different. Each birth in your life will be different. For each time you conceive, it builds up your confidence to keep birthing until you reach the final victory. However, you will notice in Genesis 29:34-35 that there was a shift in her confidence from confiding in her husband to confiding in God. **This is the season that you must confide, trust in and totally rely on God (Proverbs 3:5-6).**

The scripture says in Psalm 118:8, *"It is better to trust in the Lord than to put confidence in man."* This is why Leah said after conceiving again, "Now I will praise the Lord." Don't take it lightly your ability to conceive again. Don't even take it for granted. Many desire to give birth and can't because they have not come into the wisdom and knowledge that you have about "who" to seek first before conceiving. If God has granted you a space to conceive again, He will use it to rebuild the confidence that was weakened because of life's experiences. There is more that will be released out of you and you must push to give birth to that which will annihilate violence in your land, in your family, in your money, in your marriage, in your mind and in every aspect of your life. In essence, you cannot stop pushing because you think that you have already made great accomplishments in your marriage, in your family, and in the ministry God has given you. **There is so much more. It is time for you to go after "the so much more" in God.** You cannot stop pushing because you are unsure about the promise that God said was sure.

Most of the time women in the natural refuse to get pregnant again because of the sacrifice that is required and the death that is irrevocable. Let me make it perfectly clear, **BIRTHING IS THE LAW and since you are going to have to die anyway; you might as well die pushing out God's best!** <u>**You must be completely confident in this season that the promise is sure to all the seed.**</u> However, the scripture says in John 12:24, *"Verily, verily, I say unto you, Except a corn of wheat fall into ground and die, it abideth alone: but if it die, it bringeth forth much fruit."* The seed may look insignificant, but when it goes into the ground and dies, the release will be nothing less than much more fruit than before. **Your "yes" to the death, will bring about a "yes" to the harvest.**

While all of this bears eternal truth, I know many of you have watered and watered and watered the prophecy and the decree with your tears to the point of no return. Yet, today you still sit with no results. I discovered the end of a thing and the sure manifestation to every promise given by God. The scripture says in I Corinthians 3:5-7 in the New Living Translation, *"After all who is Apollos? Who is Paul? We are only God's servants through whom you believed the Good News. Each of us did the work the Lord gave us. I planted the seed in your hearts and Apollos watered it but it was God who made it grow. It's not important who does the planting or who does the watering.* ***What's important is that God makes the seed grow.****"* I am sure many have planted in your life, many may have even watered that which had been sown into your heart; **but it is the Almighty God who brings growth and increase to that which appears insignificant.** Anything in God that starts out as a promise will result in a fulfilled promised. Anything in God that starts out as a seed, the end result will be a harvest. God's Word does not return empty, but when it manifests, it is filled with the very substance that the individual hoped for.

The scripture in the book of Luke 1:26-35 says, *"And in the sixth month the angel Gabriel was sent from God unto a city of Galilee, named Nazareth, To a virgin espoused to a man whose name was Joseph, of the house of David; and the virgin's name was Mary. And the angel came in unto her, and said, Hail, thou that art highly favoured, the Lord is with thee: blessed art thou among women. And when she saw him, she was troubled at his saying, and cast in her mind what manner of salutation this should be. And the angel said unto her, Fear not, Mary: for thou hast found favour with God. And, behold, thou shalt conceive in thy womb, and bring forth a son, and shalt call his name JESUS. He shall be great, and shall be called the Son of the Highest: and the Lord God shall give unto him the throne of his father David: And he shall reign over the house of Jacob for ever; and of his kingdom there shall be no end. Then said Mary unto the angel, How shall this be, seeing I know not a man? And the angel answered and said unto her, The Holy Ghost shall come upon thee, and the power of the Highest shall overshadow thee: therefore also that holy thing which shall be born of thee shall be called the Son of God."* An angel came to Mary with a supernatural message. The angel told Mary that she would conceive in her womb and give birth to Jesus, the greatest miracle that ever lived. The angel told her that she would carry in her womb the Son of God and He would reign forever and of his kingdom there would be no end.

Can you imagine all of the thoughts that went through Mary's head after she received this Good News? Like many of us, she probably was perplexed because all of the odds seemed to be against her, including the fact that she was a virgin. When we look at the word *virgin,* we look at it as being someone who is having intercourse for the first time. However, if you follow me closely by the Spirit, you could pick this one up quickly without dropping it.

A *virgin* is also a person who experiences **anything for the first time**. I must make an eternal announcement to you today: There are things that have never happened to you before in the kingdom of God, a supernatural visitation has never come to some of you, debt cancellation has never happened to many of you, supernatural healing has never happened to many of you, household salvation has never happened to many of you, people have never come into your life and impacted you so quickly - that has never happened to you; the Lord has never spoken to you in an audible voice like you have long desired – that has never happened to you; and the Holy Spirit has never come upon you, like He did with Mary and caused you to bring forth…..but the Lord said to tell you that this day, an angel has been sent with the manifestation of the very thing that will **cancel your virginity**!

One of the elders in our church once said and I am going to add to what she said: "It is something about the first time in God that changes your outlook about your destiny!" Get ready for your "first time" release. It has not happened to anyone you know YET; because you will be the first. You may as well start looking for that which has never happened to you before to happen in this season. God is not slack concerning His promises. He is also not a respecter of persons. If you want your "first time" visitation, you must respond like Mary in Luke 1:38, *"....be it unto me according to thy word."*

We are in our season of the supernatural. This is the year where the Holy Spirit will govern your entrances and your exits; if you let Him. For some of you, you will experience a first time being healed by the Spirit. Some of you will experience your first time being the head and not the tail. **For some of you it will be your first time seeing God do in one day what you have been waiting on for 12 years. <u>A first time is getting ready to visit your house, saith the Lord!</u>   This is the season of the Lord's release.**

The scripture says in Deuteronomy 15:1-2, *"At the end of every seven years thou shalt make a release. And this is the manner of the release: Every creditor that lendeth ought unto his neighbour shall release it; he shall not exact it of his neighbour; or of his brother; because it is called the Lord's release."* There is nothing the enemy can do to stop a release that is called the Lord's. It is the Lord's release, but it's your harvest and mine.

After reading in I Corinthians, Chapter 3 that God brings the increase, it became eternally clear to me that **it was the Third Person of the Trinity - the Holy Spirit – the power cord of the**

Godhead that impregnated Mary <u>and caused the seed of Jesus Christ to grow within her womb.</u> It is the same Holy Spirit that will cause growth and expansion within you and bring about fruit after His own kind. Whether you realize it or not, God is after much fruit; but not just any fruit. God is after the fruit of His Spirit. The scripture says in Galatians 5:16, 22-25, *"This I say then, Walk in the Spirit, and ye shall not fulfill the lust of the flesh.....But the fruit of the Spirit is love, joy, peace, longsuffering, gentleness, goodness, faith, Meekness, temperance: against such there is no law. And they that are Christ's have crucified the flesh with the affections and lusts. If we live in the Spirit, let us also walk in the Spirit."* **If you walk in the Spirit, you will reap the benefits of the Spirit.** However, the same applies to the flesh. If you walk in the flesh, you will reap the benefits of the flesh. **It wasn't until Mary looked past her obstacles in the flesh that she was able to grab hold to what God wanted to do within her by the Spirit.**

God wants to do the impossible within you by the Spirit. However, you must first recognize that the only way a seed can go from a seed to manifested fruit is by the power of God. You must further recognize that in order to see the fruit, you must yield your members as instruments of righteousness. Why is this so important? This is important because whatever God impregnates you with is holy and cannot be treated like a normal conception or impartation.

The problem is that we have been treating this Word that is housed in our Spirit like a normal conception. However, that is a misconception. Anytime you receive a Word from the Lord, it is not a normal conception – **it's a holy thing**! When the Word of God is released, it is considered a supernatural impartation and a supernatural conception. Once released, the semen of His Word, unlike natural semen, can produce after its kind again and again and again with only one act of spiritual penetration. Only that which is holy can do such a thing.

This explains why the angel was sent to a virgin, Mary, because she had not been touched or contaminated. She was considered pure and undefiled. In essence, she was the holy and pure conduit chosen by the Father to carry a holy God (the Son of God) full-term. In her dwelled the fullness of the godhead bodily. Therefore, the scripture says in I Peter 1:15-16, *"But as he which hath called you is holy, so be ye holy in all manner of conversation; Because it is written, Be ye holy; for I am holy."* If your desire is to see manifested fruit, you must die daily to live abundantly. The scripture says in Ephesians 3:20, *"Now unto him that is able to do exceeding abundantly above all that we ask or think, according to the power that worketh in us."* If the power of

God is working on the inside of you then look for God to bring the increase from every Word spoken and every decree established. However, it shall not be by might, nor by power, but by His Spirit, saith the Lord (Zechariah 4:6).

What is your blessed assurance that the God who did it before will do it again? The scripture says in Numbers 23:19-20, *"God is not a man, that he should lie; neither the son of man, that he should repent: hath he said, and shall he not do it? or hath he spoken, and shall he not make it good? Behold, I have received commandment to bless: and he hath blessed; and I cannot reverse it."* I have read this scripture a million and one times, but not like I read it today. The scripture said that God has received commandment to bless us. He has already blessed us and it cannot be reversed. God was saying that He has already done it before and cannot go back and change the testimony of the individual who has already been blessed by His Word. Who was Mary's example? Who was Mary's testimony that God had done it before and could cause such a supernatural manifestation to take place? It was her cousin Elisabeth, who in her old age, was already six months pregnant. Elisabeth was Mary's evidence. God is speaking to you today that like Elisabeth, Tapika who they say was barren is your evidence. In Mary's case, Elisabeth already had the manifestation in her womb. Therefore, God is telling you to check

His history and check His record. The evidence is that He has already done it before!

There is nothing new under the sun. He has caused people who were barren, virgins, or those who had not had a first time, to have their first time in God. He is not a respecter of persons; look for Him to do it again! You are not the only one. There are many who went before you in the same predicament and just as God delivered them, God will deliver you. Today, ask the Holy Spirit to reveal to you your Elizabeth. This is a not gender-related. Whoever this person is male or female, they have already gone before you to make the crooked places straight and the rough places plain. Glean strength from him/her like Ruth did with Naomi and like Elisha did with Elijah and the glory of the Lord will be revealed and all flesh will see it.

Chapter 13: "Spiritual Miscarriage – What Happened to the Seed?"

"Spiritual Miscarriage – What Happened to the Seed"

I have always wondered what happens in the realm of the Spirit when a believer fails to see the full manifestation of a promise. If you are like me, questions began going through your mind like, what did I do wrong? Is God punishing me? Maybe I didn't hear from God? Or maybe I didn't receive the Word of the Lord with gladness? Whatever the question may be, there are thoughts that go through your mind, week after week, month after month, year after year, trying to figure out what happened to the seed that was planted Sunday morning in church; Tuesday afternoon in prayer; Wednesday night in Bible Study; and Thursday night at the prophetic conference. What in the world could have happened? My assignment in this chapter is to show you how although during your time in prayer, at church, bible study or where ever the Word of the Lord is heard, in an attempt to receive the Word with gladness, somehow the seed planted never reached its level of maturity. Why? It is very simple. If you are not careful in fulfilling your role as the seed-carrier, you can very easily suffer a **"Spiritual Miscarriage."**

I know we discussed some components of the word *miscarriage* in the chapter entitled, "It's Time for the Hemorrhaging to Stop". However, in an effort to ensure that I leave no opening for the enemy to roam, I found several definitions for the word *miscarriage* that will serve as a weapon against your enemy. There are two definitions that I want to point out. The first definition stated that it is the **premature** expulsion of a nonviable fetus from the uterus; also called spontaneous abortion. The second definition stated that it is the **failure of a plan**. I began to ask God, how can one mis-carry the Word of God? Then the Spirit of the Living God showed me something. He said look at the word **mis-carry.** The word *miss* is defined as, to fail to hit, reach catch, meet or accomplish. The word *carry* is defined as, to serve as a means for the conveyance of; transmit. But the definition that impressed me the most for the word *carry* said it meant to be pregnant with. The definition for the word **miscarry** given to me by the Spirit, based on these definitions, is the failed attempt to reach the end of the promise in which one was impregnated with by the Word of God. It is a type of missing the mark. I began asking the Lord how could one miscarry or spontaneously abort the Word of God once it is planted. The first thing He said was, *"Simply because they don't know how to carry the Word. They treat it like a natural seed, therefore they spend their time focusing on what they see in the natural and **mis-carry"**.* He then said to me loud and clear – *"All of which is connected to SIN. It has the ability to destroy the seed that has been planted* *although the Word of God says that the promise is sure to all the seed."*

We read earlier in a previous chapter about Romans 4:16. However, let's take a deeper look about this SURE seed to the joint-heirs of Christ. In the book of Romans 4:16-21, the scripture says, *"Therefore it is of faith, that it might be by grace; to the end the promise might be sure to all the seed; not to that only which is of the law, but to that also which is of the faith of Abraham; who is the father of us all, (As it is written, I have made thee a father of many nations,) before him whom he believed, even God, who quickeneth the dead, and calleth those things which be not as though they were. Who against hope believed in hope, that he might become the father of many nations, according to that which was spoken, So shall thy seed be. And being not weak in faith,* **he considered not his own body** *now dead, when he was about an hundred years old, neither yet the deadness of Sarah's womb: He staggered not at the promise of God through unbelief; but was strong in faith, giving glory to God; And being fully persuaded that, what he had promised, he was able also to perform."* The scripture says that the promise is SURE to ALL the seed. In essence, the end result will be manifested based upon the seed that was planted by faith. However, because the seed was planted by faith, in order for it to continue to grow and develop it must endure until the end by faith. Does that make sense? Sure it does.

In Romans, Chapter 4, in verse 19 it says that Abraham was not weak in faith, nor did he consider his own body, that appeared to be naturally incapable of carrying a seed. Neither did he consider the deadness of Sarah's womb. Abraham staggered not at the promises. He was not persuaded by circumstances. He was FULLY persuaded that God would comply with the covenant. He was strong in faith, **giving glory to God** for something he could not see, yet he believed. Let me say something right here. God does not want us talking to Him about the things we can see. He wants us to speak from the position of faith and talk to Him about the things we can't see! Abraham was willing to carry the seed that was planted by faith. He was fully (totally and completely) persuaded. What am I saying to you? If you are not fully persuaded today about what God promised you, you have not reached the realm in which He desires for you to see the promise manifested. Yes, I know that is a very strong statement. However, Abraham was used as an example for the believer that we might inherit the promises of God by faith. This is the reason why he was called a father to us all.

In Galatians 3:29, the scripture says, *"And if ye be Christ's, then are ye Abraham's seed, and heirs according to the promise."* God wants us to trust Him **in spite of what occurs after** we have heard the Word about the situation. According to the New Living translation, the scripture says in Proverbs 3:5-6, *"Trust in the Lord with all your heart;* **do not depend on your own understanding.** *Seek his will in all you do, and he will direct your paths."* You cannot depend on your own understanding. It will fail you every time. However, God's understanding is complete. The scripture says in Philippians 1:6, He started a work to finish it and perform it. You must believe that He will do nothing less than finish what He started in your life!

The problem believers have is when things start to look dead, **instead of giving God the glory, we begin to fall short of His glory** by doubting based on what we see. In Romans 3:23, the scripture says, *"For all have sinned, and come short of the glory of God."* In essence, we begin to doubt God's ability to perform a resurrection on what appears to be a dead situation. For those of you who are not aware, doubt is sin. As mentioned in a previous chapter, sin is defined as missing the mark, as well as, **anything** that separates you from the plan, purpose and presence of God. If there is **anything** or **anyone** that is causing you to become separated from the plan, purpose and presence of God flee from them. Unconfessed sin has the ability to separate you from God's plan and the end result could be a **"Spiritual Miscarriage"**.

In John 15:4-5 the scripture says, *"Abide in me, and I in*

you. As the branch cannot bear fruit of itself, except it abide in the vine; no more can ye, except ye abide in me. I am the vine, ye are the branches: He that abideth in me, and I in him, the same bringeth forth much fruit: for without me ye can do nothing." Unless you remain connected to the vine, you will suffer a **"Spiritual Miscarriage"** every time there is a conception. Every time you receive a prophecy, every time you hear a word in bible study or at a Sunday morning service, UNLESS YOU CONSISTENTLY REMAIN ATTACHED TO THE SEED PLANTER, YOU WILL MISCARRY EVERY TIME! We fail to realize that any form of disconnection from God, no matter what shape or form it comes in is SIN.

Let me take it another step further so that you can have a clear understanding of what God is saying. You can **mis-carry** when you operate in fear. How? Because you have separated yourself from the scripture that says in II Timothy 1:7, *"For God hath not given us the spirit of fear; but of power, and of love, and a sound mind."* You can **mis-carry** when you don't pray. How? Because you have separated yourself from the scripture that says in I Thessalonians 5:17, *"Pray without ceasing."* You can **mis-carry** when you don't love your neighbor as yourself. How? Because you have separated yourself from the scripture that says in I John 4:11, *"Beloved, if God so loved us, we ought also to love one* *another."* You can **mis-carry** when you don't tithe. How? Because you have separated yourself from the scripture in Malachi 3:10 that says, *"Bring ye all the tithes into the storehouse, that there may be meat in mine house, and prove me now herewith.....if I will not open you the windows of heaven and pour you out a blessing, that there shall not be room enough to receive it."* But one of the main reasons I believe that many believers **mis-carry** in their finances is because we separate ourselves from the tithing scripture in verse 10. Therefore, verse 11 cannot be implemented.

In Malachi 3:11, the scripture says, *"And I will rebuke the devourer for your sakes, and he shall not destroy the fruits of your ground; neither shall your vine cast her fruit before* (prematurely) *the time in the field, saith the Lord of hosts."* Many of you are experiencing **"Spiritual Miscarriages"** simply because of disobedience. You allow yourself to become uncovered when you disobey the Word of the Lord. The only way you can **re-cover** is if you repent and confess your faults before God, as it states in I John 1:9. DO NOT WALLOW IN SIN. YOU MUST QUICKLY REPENT, CONFESS IT AND MOVE ON!

As we close this chapter, in the book of Hosea 9:9-14, there is divine revelation about what happens when one separates themselves from the plan, purpose and presence of the Almighty God. The scripture says, *"They have deeply corrupted themselves, as in the days of Gibeah: therefore he will remember their iniquity, he will visit their sins. I found Israel like grapes in the wilderness; I saw your fathers as the firstripe in the fig tree at her first time: but they went to Baal-peor, and* **separated themselves** *unto that shame; and their abominations were according as they loved.* I mentioned verse 14 in the book of Hosea, Chapter 9 earlier. However, it is well worth repeating for further revelation. It says, *"Give them, O Lord: what wilt thou give? give them a miscarrying womb and dry breasts."* Any type of separation from God could cause you to suffer a ***"Spiritual Miscarriage."*** Therefore, I admonish you, no matter what situation occurs, you must stand still and know that He is the God of all promises. He will bring to pass what He spoke. He is faithful to watch over His Word to perform it. However, you must fulfill your responsibility as the seed carrier. You MUST stay connected to the true vine or your branches will become separated and die.

Today, assess where you are in God, if there be any un-confessed sin among you – deal with it QUICKLY! This is between you and God. If you want to experience the ***"Birthing Process"*** in its entirety you must doubt not, be fully persuaded and most importantly – MAINTAIN YOUR RELATIONSHIP WITH THE GIVER OF LIFE – JESUS CHRIST! God knows where you are. He is an omnipresent God. His presence does not come and go. He is ever present (Psalm 139:1-3). However, in order for you to experience the manifested presence of God, you must seek Him to find the treasure that He has promised. He wants you to experience His fullness, but you must seek first the kingdom of God and His righteousness. As well as, remain attached to the King of kings in order to see the benefits of the kingdom manifested in every area of your life!

THE THIRD TRIMESTER

Natural Law: In medicine, in the Third Trimester the mother's final weight gain takes place and the fetus begins to move regularly. This period of pregnancy can be uncomfortable, causing symptoms like weak bladder control and backache. Movement of the fetus becomes stronger and more frequent and the fetus prepares for viability outside the womb through improved brain, eye and muscle function. The mother can feel the baby "rolling" and it may cause pain or discomfort when the baby is in the mother's ribs. Because this takes place during the $7^{th} - 9^{th}$ months, the mother's womb is running out of space; which is visible evidence that the baby's entry is near.

Spiritual Law: It is during this time when you know that the manifestation of the promise is near. Your territory has been enlarged, you are in the final stretch and you are voiding out every form of liquid. It is simply because you are no more a babe in Christ; but one that is on strong meat. Now you must be careful not to ingest anything that you can't digest properly; due to the possibilities of indigestion because of lack of space. However, it is also the time when the spirit of weariness comes upon you. The weight and wait of the promise causes you to become tired and anxious. But this is when you must loose the spirit of fear from you. Because you have made your request known unto God, the evidence that the time of your delivery is near is because the opposition within you has intensified!

Chapter 14: "Braxton-Hicks – False Contractions"

"Braxton-Hicks – False Contractions"

This may be one of the most profound chapter's in the book, because it provides insight to what God calls "light afflictions". In medical terms, *Braxton-Hicks* are described as sporadic uterine contractions that actually start beginning as early as 6 weeks. Although one may not feel them that early, most women start feeling them during the second or third trimester of pregnancy. *Braxton-Hicks* contractions are the tightening of the uterine muscles for one to two minutes and are thought to be an aid to the body in preparation for birth. However, as I researched further, I realized that not all mothers have these contractions. These contractions are thought to be part of the process of effacement, the thinning and dilation of the cervix. Normally, doctors provide several solutions to relieve these contractions. They include: changing positions, taking a warm bath or shower, drinking water, resting, or changing activities. How does this relate to the believer today? I believe that there are times as Believers that we think that the promise is near based on the pain we are feeling. However, each tightening or stretching of our faith will not result in the promise. As a matter of fact, seeing that the promise is already prepared for us, the false contractions are necessary to prepare us for the promise.

Let's look at another aspect of Abraham, Sarah and Hagar. Hagar was the first single mother in the Bible. However, it was unfortunate because she was used as a shortcut to the promise. In the book of Genesis, Chapter 15, God told Abraham (at the time his name was Abram) that a son would come through his bowels. However, there appeared to be one obstacle, Sarah (at the time her name was Sarai), his wife, had been restrained by the Lord from bearing children (Genesis 16:2).

The scripture says in Genesis 16:1-6, *"Now Sarai Abram's wife bare him no children: and she had an handmaid, an Egyptian, whose name was Hagar. And Sarai said unto Abram, Behold now, the Lord hath restrained me from bearing: I pray thee, go in unto my maid; it may be that I may obtain children by her. And Abram hearkened to the voice of Sarai. And Sarai Abram's wife took Hagar her maid the Egyptian after Abram had dwelt ten years in the land of Canaan, and gave her to her husband Abram to be his wife. And he went in unto Hagar and she conceived: and when she saw that she had conceived, her mistress was despised in her eyes. And Sarai said unto Abram, My wrong be upon tee: I have given my maid into thy bosom; and when she saw that she had conceived, I was despised in her eyes: the Lord judge between me and thee. But Abram said unto Sarai, Behold, thy maid is in thy hand; do to her as it pleaseth thee. And when*

Sarai dealt hardly with her, she fled from her face." Sarah's pain of not being able to have a child caused her to implement her own plan by including her handmaiden, Hagar. Yet, this was neither the conception nor the birth that God intended for Abraham and Sarah. This conception was Sarah's plan, not God's and every plan of the flesh will experience consequences of the flesh. The scripture says in Galatians 6:8, *"For he that soweth to his flesh shall of the flesh reap corruption..."* Little did Abraham and Sarah know that they had sowed in the flesh and of the flesh would they reap.

In Sarah's own mind, I believe she thought once Hagar conceived the pain or contractions that were coming from the void of having a child would go away. However, she complicated an issue because nothing can fill a space that God caused to be empty for a season. In essence, there is no replacement for what God promised. Although you may experience pain and discomfort during this journey of the birthing process that does not mean it is time to locate a surrogate. There is no back-up plan in God. He knows the plans He has for you. His plans include thoughts of good and not of evil, to bring you into an expected end (Jeremiah 29:11). The *Braxton-Hicks* are meant to familiarize you with what is to come. They are the light affliction that God will use to launch you into the realm of the unseen. *Braxton-Hicks* are a temporary affliction that only lasts for a moment but at the end, will result in an exceeding and eternal weight of glory. Therefore, you must endure the false contractions of life until God brings the increase. Let's take a look at David. He had several "Braxton-Hicks" before reaching his "Goliath" destination. In the book of I Samuel 17:34-37, the scripture says, *"And David said unto Saul, Thy servant kept his father's sheep, and there came a lion, and a bear, and took a lamb out of the flock: And I went out after him, and smote him, and delivered it out of his mouth: and when he arose against me, I caught him by his beard, and smote him, and slew him. Thy servant slew both the lion and the bear: and this uncircumcised Philistine shall be as one of them, seeing he hath defied the armies of the living God. David said moreover, The LORD that delivered me out of the paw of the lion, and out of the paw of the bear, he will deliver me out of the hand of this Philistine. And Saul said unto David, Go, and the LORD be with thee."* David killed a lion and a bear. Both of these incidents were prerequisites for what was to come – Goliath. The lion and the bear were used to build David's faith. Thus, when David heard about the uncircumcised Philistine, Goliath, he was FULLY PERSUADED that he could overthrow him. What point am I making? The Braxton-Hicks are preparation for the delivery of a lifetime. They are used to prepare you for the next level in glory. They are used to fulfill the process and thrust you into the end of the thing that God promised. I have always been intrigued by the conception of Jesus Christ by the Holy Ghost in Mary's womb. However, what is most intriguing is the salutation at the door when Mary and Elizabeth's wombs meet for the first time. The scripture says in the book of Luke 1:41-45, *"And it came to pass, that, when Elisabeth heard the salutation of Mary, the babe leaped in her womb; and Elisabeth was filled with the Holy Ghost: And she spake out with a loud voice, and said, Blessed art thou among women, and blessed is the fruit of thy womb. And whence is this to me, that the mother of my Lord should come to me? For, lo, as soon as the voice of thy salutation sounded in mine ears, the babe leaped in my womb for joy. And blessed is she that believed: for there shall be a performance of those things which were told her from the Lord."* As soon as Elisabeth heard Mary's greeting, the infant leaped in her womb. Now that is what I call real Braxton-Hicks. This should be the norm for every believer that comes into contact with another believer. The Holy Ghost in me should activate something in you. That activation should serve as a confirmation that there shall be a performance of things in both of us. Elisabeth was pregnant with John and Mary had just become impregnated by the Holy Ghost with Jesus Christ. The baby leaped in Elisabeth's womb because John would be the one who would go before Jesus Christ to prepare the way of His coming. I told you earlier that the *Braxton-*

Hicks are used to prepare your body for the birth of a lifetime. The Spirit of the Lord sent Mary to Elisabeth's door to confirm that someone greater is coming – prepare the way. There are many of you who will experience a Mary and Elizabeth moment as you are reading this part of the book. God will show you that what you have carried with His name is not inactive; it has life and life more abundantly. Therefore, look for a performance of those things which have been told you by the Lord. In the book of I Samuel, Chapter 1, Hannah was experiencing spiritual Braxton-Hicks that were caused by her frustration with Peninah. The scripture says in I Samuel 1:4-7, *"And when the time was that Elkanah offered, he gave to Peninnah his wife, and to all her sons and her daughters, portions: But unto Hannah he gave a worthy portion; for he loved Hannah: but the Lord had shut up her womb. And her adversary also provoked her sore, for to make her fret, because the Lord had shut up her womb. And as he did so year by year, when she went up to the house of the Lord, so she provoked her; therefore she wept, and did not eat."* The scripture said that Peninnah provoked Hannah. This meant that Peninnah aggravated Hannah and caused her to be uncomfortable because what Peninnah had, Hannah desired. There may be times when people will give birth before you, but you must not allow their release to frustrate the plan that God has for you. Your turn will come. However, frustration, jealousy or envy will delay the harvest you have long awaited.

In the book of Exodus 1:15-21, the scripture says in the Amplified Bible, *"Then Pharaoh, the king of Egypt, gave this order to the Hebrew midwives, Shiphrah and Puah: "When you help the Hebrew women as they give birth, watch as they deliver. If the baby is a boy, kill him; if it is a girl, let her live." But because the midwives feared God, they refused to obey the king's orders. They allowed the boys to live, too. So the king of Egypt called for the midwives. "Why have you done this?" he demanded. "Why have you allowed the boys to live?" "The Hebrew women are not like the Egyptian women," the midwives replied. "They are more vigorous and have their babies so quickly that we cannot get there in time." So God was good to the midwives, and the Israelites continued to multiply, growing more and more powerful. And because the midwives feared God, he gave them families of their own."* First, the word *midwife* is defined as a person trained to assist women in childbirth. However, another definition that caught my attention was: One who produces or aids in producing something new. When I desired a baby, one of the things that I learned was the power of intercession. Although I desired a baby for myself, what pleased God the most was my willingness to lay aside my desire and pick up someone else's. **Before you give birth to anything of your own in God, you must first learn the**

principle of being a midwife for someone else.

Shiphrah and Puah were given an order by Pharaoh to kill all the male children and allow the female children to live. However, they refused because they feared God more than man. Therefore, they allowed the boys to live once they were delivered. When the women were asked why they refused to follow the orders given by Pharaoh, they basically said, and I will paraphrase, *"The Hebrew women are a peculiar people, they don't deliver like everyone else. Their deliveries are different. As a matter of fact, before she travails, she brings forth; before her pain comes, she is delivered of a man child (Isaiah 66:7)."* I began thinking, if the Hebrew women deliver before they travail and before the pain comes, then what is the purpose of the midwife? Sometimes God will have you in the right place, at the right time to intercede for someone else just to get you the desires of your heart.

The scripture says in Galatians 6:7-9, *"Be not deceived; God is not mocked: for whatsoever a man soweth, that shall he also reap. For he that soweth to his flesh shall of the flesh reap corruption; but he that soweth to the Spirit shall of the Spirit reap life everlasting. And let us not be weary in well doing: for in due season we shall reap, if we faint not."* According to the divine systems of protocol, whatever a man sows that is what he will reap. When I sowed prayers of fruitfulness into the barren wombs of those 30 women God instructed me to intercede for, I reaped fruitfulness in my own womb. God is not a man that He should lie. He is bound to His Word and it cannot return void. The same thing happened to Shiphrah and Puah in Exodus, Chapter 1. They were faithful in assisting the Hebrew women in their time of birthing. Therefore, the Lord gave Shiphrah and Puah families too.

If you ever want breakthrough in any area that seems insurmountable, ask the Lord to show you individuals who need breakthrough in the same area and serve as their midwife. This will cause a massive explosion of the manifested promises of God in your life, as well as the life of the person you pray for. However, let me warn you, more will be required of you. As you speak life to their circumstances, there will be a death taking place on your end. Like me, I did not see immediate results. As I mentioned earlier, the women that I was instructed to pray for were getting pregnant, some with multiples. Yet, I was still barren in the natural, but not in my Spirit. I understood the power of intercession and the relevance of calling those things that be not as though they were made a mark in the realm of the spirit that could not be erased.

What point am I making? Just because you experience some discomfort does not mean it is time to push. It simply means that the stretching or the discomfort is preparing you for what is next in the birthing process.

Chapter 15: "The Labor Pains and the Gift"

"The Labor Pains and the Gift"

I realized my full assignment in God during the process of writing this book. It is to take you out of your comfort zone. It is time for you, the Body of Christ, to come out from among them and be ye separate. We shouldn't look, respond or act like any other people. We are of a different culture. The culture of the kingdom of God is peculiar; it is royal and sometimes without definition it is so expansive. Yet, as a member of the commonwealth society of the Kingdom of God, we have not been in our rightful positions to advance the agenda of the Kingdom. I'm not speaking from what I heard, but from experience.

In December 2006, the Lord instructed my husband and I that it was time for me to leave my full-time job. What a difficult time in God this would be for me. I kept hearing something in the room as I was walking the floor, and I want you to hear me by the Spirit. The Spirit of the Lord said that it is time for you to engage. Many Believers have been disengaged from the society in which they were born. Therefore, when the Lord gives an assignment it is very difficult for many to carry it out because they have aligned themselves to this temporary culture and temporary way of life instead of the eternal culture from which they were derived. The Body of Christ whether we realize it or not, for years have been actively disengaged from our purpose.

There was a study conducted in the Gallup Management Journal in 2001 regarding the "Actively Disengaged" employees those who have fundamentally disconnected from their jobs. The study discussed in detail how those individuals cost the U. S. economy between $292 billion and $355 billion a year. According to this study, there are 24.7 million workers that are actively disengaged in the U.S. workforce. The study further discovered that actively disengaged workers tend to be significantly less productive, report being less loyal to their companies, are less satisfied with their personal lives, and are more stressed and insecure about their work than their colleagues. Not to include they miss an average 3.5 more days per year than other workers do or 86.5 million days in all. What are we doing? The research finally concluded that 29% of the U.S. workforce is actively engaged, 55% is not engaged, and 16% is actively disengaged. In other words, 71% of Americans who go to work every day are not engaged in their jobs.

According to Gallup's study the "engaged" employees are builders who use their talents and develop productive relationships. The employees that are "not engaged" tend toward indifference. They take a wait-and-see attitude toward their work, their employer and their peers. They do not initiate and move the organization forward. Finally, the "actively disengaged" feel and act out estrangement from the organization. This is truly poisonous for productivity. Why did I take time to say all of that? Some of the people in the church are beginning to look just like the world; we lack productivity. This was never God's intent. I believe by the Spirit that this book will encourage a visitation from on High and a dynamic paradigm shift. It will be a move of God that will catapult you into your divine assignment and destiny. As this Word is released you will be provoked to action. As a matter of fact, I feel like the angel in John, Chapter 5, who stepped into the pool of Bethesda, to trouble the water and cause activation within the people.

In John 5:2-9 in the Amplified Bible, the scripture says, *"Now there is in Jerusalem a pool near the Sheep Gate. This pool in the Hebrew is called Bethesda, having five porches (alcoves, colonnades, doorways). In these lay a great number of sick folk— some blind, some crippled, and some paralyzed (shriveled up)- waiting for the bubbling up of the water. For an angel of the Lord went down at appointed seasons into the pool and moved and stirred up the water; whoever then first, after the stirring up of the water, stepped in was cured of whatever disease with which he was afflicted. There was a certain man there who had suffered with a deep-seated and lingering disorder for thirty-eight years. When*

Jesus noticed him lying there [helpless], knowing that he had already been a long time in that condition, He said to him, Do you want to become well? [Are you really in earnest about getting well?] The invalid answered, Sir, I have nobody when the water is moving to put me into the pool; but while I am trying to come [into it] myself, somebody else steps down ahead of me. Jesus said to him, Get up! Pick up your bed (sleeping pad) and walk! Instantly the man became well and recovered his strength and picked up his bed and walked. But that happened on the Sabbath." These folk were waiting for some spectacular phenomenon to fall from the sky, I guess like some of us. They were waiting on the water to speak, so that they could come out of their captivity. God is saying, just like He said to the man who had been there in that same predicament for 38 long years, "You are no longer waiting on me. I am waiting on you to just step in!" When you step in you will be made whole in every area of your life.

    What I thought was most important about the book of John, Chapter 5, was in verse 18. The scripture says in John 5:18 in the Amplified Version, *"This made the Jews more determined than ever to kill Him [to do away with Him]; because He not only was breaking (weakening, violating) the Sabbath, but He actually was speaking of God as being [in a special sense] His own Father, making Himself equal [putting Himself on a level] with God."*

They wanted to kill Jesus because He was operating in His gift. You need to know that as you operate in gift that God has called you to persecution will arise. People who you thought were close to you will act differently and the enemy will tell you that it is your fault. Some of them may even walk away and leave you. You may be like Tonto without the Lone Ranger; but those who live, according to the precepts of this heavenly counsel, shall without a doubt, suffer persecution.

There is a death required of you to walk in your divine assignment. Some of you have been in a wrestling match like Jacob was with the angel in Genesis, Chapter 32. I know, because I was having that same wrestling match when God instructed me to do Barren Breaking Ministry Fellowships. I remember feeling like Jonah one day. I knew what direction God wanted me to go, but was hesitant because of what it would cost me to get there. It wasn't that like many of you I didn't know I was called. I knew I was called to do great things for God a long time ago. But it was because of the intense death that would be required to carry out the assignment.

One day, I remember saying to the Lord, "If I die anymore they will have to bury me." The Lord's response to me was *"Daughter that is exactly what I want – I want YOU to be buried so the gift that is in you can be birthed and resurrected in its fullness."* In the book of John 12:24, the scripture says, *"Except a corn of wheat fall into the ground and die, it abideth alone: but if it die, it bringeth forth much fruit."* If you are going to carry out your kingdom assignment – death is required of how you think, what you think the kingdom is and your traditional, religious occupancy of how things should operate – because that is the norm. If you want to bring forth much fruit, death is required and not optional. There are many assignments that God has given unto each of us. Some of them cannot vividly be explained. In some instances – it almost makes no sense to the hearer. So if we are going to walk in these things it will require a dead man's faith. What is a dead man's faith – He is a man that has absolutely nothing else to lose.

Several years ago, in my prayer journal I documented an account of a vision that I saw. It was a very graphic interpretation of births that were taking place. However, I saw no womb-yet I knew they were coming from a canal. But what I saw were bloody babies. They were on an assembly line being birthed quickly. There were doctors in blue scrubs with white masks passing the babies one by one to one another as they were coming out of the birth canal. Some of the doctors were at the end of the assembly line cleaning the babies off and wrapping them in white linen blankets in preparation for others to see the gift from God that had come forth. After seeing this vision, its interpretation was not clear enough to discuss until God opened up the revelation. You must recognize that the labor pains will always last longer than the birth because of the weight, height and depth of the baby. This confirms the reason why I saw no womb because the pains had finally passed for the gift to be delivered. Therefore, where the babies were coming from really didn't matter because the pain that God uses as a midwife to get the promise or the gift here were over. What point am I making? The pain is scheduled to pass so that the gift and the promise can be delivered. However, this time, you must yield to the delivery.

A natural baby cannot be born without the direct cooperation of the mother. God wants to bring to the birth in your life in one day, what it took many years for others to obtain (Isaiah 66:8). This is the year that God will finish what He started but you must yield and not be bound by tradition. I have found that when God wants to deliver His best, His mechanism to do so is through pain. It is the Believers midwife. If you know anything about a woman in the delivery room, pain is one of the things in which the doctors use to calculate the arrival of the promise.

The scripture says in I Corinthians 12:4-5, that there are diversities of gifts, but the same Spirit and there are differences in administration, but the same Lord. But in that same chapter in verse 18 in the New Living translation, the scripture says, *"But God made our bodies with many parts, and he has put each part just where he wants it."* Each part supplies its sufficient amount to the body. All of which makes up an effective body. Therefore, each gift is necessary in the kingdom of God. But this is the key, I am your midwife and you are mine. What God has assigned for me to do in the kingdom right now should not stir up envy and strife – it should stir up the gift.

The gifts and calling of God (Romans 11:29) should cause an expectation to leap in your womb, even as Elisabeth did with Mary. It should cause something in you to react because we are a body that should be fitly joined together. The weight of your baby may not be the weight of my baby. However, God has placed in each of us a gift. Your pain may not even be as intense as mine. However, there is something in each of us that requires pain so that a birth can take place. When a woman is in labor, the more intense the pain becomes, the more she expands or what the doctors call dilate. It is the expanding of the cervix to make room for the mother to give birth to the gift in which she is carrying. She cannot give birth in the normal manner until she is at the height of her pain and she has completely dilated to 10 centimeters.

Your true value and worth in the kingdom will remain hidden until you find out the real treasure that lies deep within your earthen vessel. The scripture says in II Corinthians 4:7, *"But we have this treasure in earthen vessels, that the excellency of the power may be of God, and not of us."* There is a treasure within you that lies deep beneath the surface. It is sometimes a treasure that lies beneath much debris. I am reminded of something the Lord told me a couple of months ago. The soil in the ground is like the soul. Until it is broken up it cannot receive the seed. What am I saying? The reason why many cannot cooperate with the kingdom of God is due to the debris that has yet to be removed from within. The contaminated debris in a believer's heart has the ability to make the seed ineffective and inoperative. We discussed some of this in an earlier chapter. When the Word of God is released, it must fall on good ground in order to produce after its kind (Matthew 13:3-9). If you desire to cooperate with the kingdom of God, you must ensure that every time a Word is released in your life, it is falling on good ground. What is good ground? A repented soul is good ground.

The treasure within your earthen vessel is the greatest asset and investment given unto you as a Believer. I believe that there is schism in the body of Christ simply because of our own inabilities to operate in the very thing we were created to do. We find it comfortable to operate in an area where we can see a paycheck from week to week. Ask me how I know? But when the Lord wants to release you from the common into that which is kingdom-oriented, kingdom-birthed, and kingdom-breathed, your entire mindset must switch from what many call a talent to what God calls your purposed gift. When you refuse to yield to this type of kingdom release, you will limit your potential every single day until you make a kingdom-conscious decision to make the change from seeing it to knowing it. The scripture says in I John 5:14, *"....this is the confidence that we have in him, that, if we ask any thing according to his will, he heareth us."* This is where I am today, CONFIDENT in Him. I know I am in my right place in the kingdom. I am no longer out of place, because where I am is a perfect fit. Though some days can be highly uncomfortable knowing that your steps have been ordered by God is the only security I need.

When you only operate in your talent, it provides a response from the audience. But when you operate in your gift, you may not ever receive a response, yet you reap an eternal reward. The scripture says in Proverbs 18:16, *"A man's gift maketh room for him and bringeth him before great men."* While the talent may render applause, the gift will make room for you and set you in an even larger place than you were before. There are some talented performances that never go on the road because the audience demand wasn't so great. However, when it's a gift, something that is given freely, people will show up and receive it, simply because they didn't have to pay anything to get it. There are no restrictions with the gift. Jesus afforded us the best gift ever, eternal life. This is an irreplaceable gift. There is not enough money or things that can recompense for such a gift. As a matter of fact, a gift is something bestowed voluntarily and without compensation. But if you pay the right price, you can see a person's talent in full operation. Although there is a form of payment required to see the fullness of who God has called you to be. When you see the harvest (souls, deliverance, healings and all else) it will be well worth it!

The scripture says in Proverbs 17:8, *"A gift is as a precious stone in the eyes of him that hath it: whithersoever it turneth, it prospereth."* Whenever you begin to recognize and acknowledge the gift that God has given you, it will turn EVERY area of your life in the direction of the promise. How am I so sure? The scripture says in Romans 11:29, *"For the gifts and calling of God are without repentance."* No matter how you turn it, it must move in the direction of the promise. It cannot return void. It will make room for you in every area of your life. Hypothetically, your talent may open a window, but your gift will open up doors for you that no man can shut. I want you to hear the Lord speaking to you clearly, as if He is sitting down having a one on one conversation with you. You will not see the fullness of the promise until you find out, locate, and single out the gift that is living within you. Your inheritance, your children's inheritance, and all else will be unleashed as you walk in what God has ordained for you, not someone else.

You see people operating in their gift every day on television. Whether it is in the area of talk show host, sports, singing, dancing, acting and many others they excelled because they tapped into the gift without hesitation. They focused on the area where they knew they were strong and developed that area. Are you hearing me by the Spirit? Focus on your area of strength and let the Lord reveal to you His plan, direction and divine purpose for your life. It is time for the believer's to learn how to cooperate with the kingdom of God by doing, not just hearing!

The scripture says in Romans 2:13, *"(For not the hearers of the law are just before God, but the doers of the law shall be justified.)"* The scripture also says in James 1:22, *"But be ye doers of the word, and not hearers only, deceiving your own selves."* Wow, that is Rhema! God is saying you are deceiving yourself if you have continuously heard this Word preached and still are in the same place, doing the same thing. In essence, to God you are not justified until you begin to put feet to what you have heard. My prayer has simply been that the Lord would help people make a kingdom-conscious decision to walk out what they have already heard over and over and over again.

I have found as I travel, that many are still searching, not seeking, other mechanisms to fill their God-shaped hole. Let me help you, nothing will fill that void but God. Therefore, when He comes to fill it, it will be filled with what He has assigned for you. Not what you want to do. It is time to release you into your moments of destiny. Don't miss the moment because of fear or as I always say, lack of evidence. Some of you will have multiple births. When you yield to the Spirit of God and allow His Word to impregnate you, you become a candidate for consistent and timely births. However, what is taking place right now is the thing that happens in between the labor pains and the birth. It is called TRAVAIL.

The scripture says in the book of Micah 4:9-10, *"Now why dost thou cry out aloud? is there no king in thee? is thy counselor perished? for pangs have taken thee as a woman in travail. Be in pain, and labour to bring forth, O daughter of Zion, like a woman in travail: for now shalt thou go forth out of the city, and thou shalt dwell in the field, and thou shalt go even to Babylon;* **there shalt thou be delivered***; there the Lord shall redeem thee from the hand of thine enemies."* You have not been hurting or in pain for nothing. It is simply so that you can give birth to the fullness that

He has put on the inside of you. The pain was the prerequisite for the delivery. The pain was the prerequisite for you to bring forth a king – the King of kings, who represents a kingdom; the kingdom of God. If there is a king in you, there is a kingdom in you. If there is a king in you, the pain and suffering may not be minimal. This explains why Micah replied in Micah 4:9-10 according to the New Living Translation, *"....why are you now screaming in terror? Have you no king to lead you?"* You have read more than once in this book that Christ in you is the fullness and the hope of glory. If Christ is in you, the pain is required to expel out of you every other tenant and make known what has been hid for generations.

    Let me make mention of this before moving further. In the book of Micah, Chapter 4, Micah reveals the place where you shall be delivered or give birth; that place is in Babylon. Babylon is known as the place of "confusion". What point am I making? Don't look for the delivery of your business, ministry, or anything else God has promised you to take place in a peaceable, pretty and comfortable place. The only begotten Son, Jesus, was born in the worst circumstance, in a manger. I can only imagine that there had to be fragrances in this manger that did not reflect His deity nor was there a parade or an entourage to celebrate His coming. Yet, there the promise of the only begotten Son lay in a barn, in a manger, which was described as some type of stall or crib for feeding cattle.

Jesus, the King of kings and Lord of lords, was wrapped in swaddling clothing lying in a manger. This to me is considered to be a very unusual place for a King. As a matter of fact, it could be confusing to some. Yet, the condition in which He was birthed did not deter His royalty or the position in which He was eternally birthed. I believe that too many times as believers we allow our natural circumstances to determine the barometer, measure and proximity as to how close or how far we are from what God purposed. Here is a spiritual nugget for you. You cannot determine the value of the release, the timing of the release nor the proximity of the release based upon what it is wrapped in! Your release may be wrapped in a season of confusion. Your release may be wrapped in a season of barrenness. Your release may be wrapped in a season of sickness. Your release may be wrapped in days and months of total disappointment, discouragement and doubt. However, hear me by the Spirit. Don't be fooled, because the very thing it is wrapped in is the delivery system that God will use to get you to the place He promised.

The scripture says in Psalm 48:6, *"Fear took hold upon them there, and pain, as of a woman in travail."* Fear has traumatized and paralyzed many of you so much that you are afraid to take one step in God. It is a trick of the enemy to get you stuck in your talent, so that you will never give birth to the gift. Some of you are simply afraid of what might happen "if". The devil has poured out the "what-if" spirit on you. You must take authority over the "what-ifs" because the scripture says in Hebrews 11:1, NOW FAITH IS!

God not only desires for the gift to come forth – it is much greater than that. According to Philippians 4:17, the scripture says, *"Not because I desire a gift: but I desire fruit that may abound to your account."* God is simply trying to get something to you by what will come through you. It is the gifts and calling of God. This next move is not just about you, it will impact nations. Look at the lives of Esther, Mary, Moses, and Elisha. There are many examples, including Jesus Himself, who operated in the gift and caused an eternal impact on multitudes of people. It is the kind of impact that is still producing after His kind today. It is the time of productivity in the kingdom of God. Our season of barrenness has come to an official end. No more hearing and not doing. It's time to put your feet in the stirrups and release the manifestation of the prophecy. It is time for all to see that the stretching was not in vain.

The scripture says in Isaiah 49:20, *"The children which thou shalt have, after thou hast lost the other, shall say again in thine ears, The place is too strait for me: give place to me that I may dwell."* The place where you are is too narrow to give birth to the gift. An expansion must take place in order for it to come forth. Your mindset must be expanded. Some of you are thinking way below sea level. You cannot have a grasshopper mentality in your season of birthing (Numbers 13:33). When you are a carrier of the King of kings, you cannot carry thoughts of inadequacy and expect kingdom results. The scripture says in Proverbs 23:7 in the Amplified Version, *"For as he thinks in his heart, so is he."* You must choose to think on those things that are pure, that are just and that are of a good report. You must think on those things that you have learned from the Spirit of the Living God, then the God of peace will be with you (Philippians 4:8-9).

In Isaiah 37:3, the scripture says, *"...for the children are come to the birth, and there is not strength to bring forth."* The scripture is simply saying that YES it is time to deliver. However, there is not enough strength in the carrier to push it out. I told you at the beginning of this book that I am your assigned midwife. If a spiritual caesarean section or C-section is required, fear not, the Word of God will bring the increase. Thus, the end result is that you will give birth. It's been way too long and no more time will be afforded to you. The time is right now! The Spirit of the Lord released this chapter of the book according to II Timothy 1:6 to stir up the gift that is within you. It has been lying dormant for way too long. It is time for it to speak and not lie, saith the Lord! There are even some visions and dreams that have not come to pass because you have refused to operate in the gift that will make that dream or vision a reality. Despite the delay, yours days shall be no more prolonged. This is the day that the Lord has made for you to birth out the gift that will cause fruitfulness to manifest in every area of your life.

Chapter 16: Stage 1 – Early Labor, Active Labor and Transitioning

"Stage 1 - Early Labor, Active Labor and Transitioning"

There are three stages in the actual birthing process. The first stage is known as **Early Labor, Active Labor and Transitioning**. Stage 2 is known as Pushing and Stage 3 is known as the Delivery of the Placenta. Now man of God, before you convince yourself that this book does not apply to you, hold on to your seat. This is a Word for the Body of Christ and I declare in the name of Jesus that every eye reading it will be open to what God is doing in their respective lives right now. This Word will cause you to look at where you are so differently and receive the birthing process that has been ordained of God with gladness. The voice that goes beyond reason has impressed upon me to drop this in your spirit before I continue. Read slowly and carefully, every word you hear and read in this season is critical and God doesn't want you to miss one word. Here you go: *You are not far from your land of promise; the enemy lied again. You are on the verge of giving birth to the greatest harvest you have ever laid your eyes on. As a matter of fact, you are in the delivery room RIGHT NOW! However, don't push just yet, for there are stages to this birthing process and you must endure all three stages to give birth to this new thing that I have ordained. This is the new* *thing that I promised you years ago. Yet, the birthing is not like any other birth you have experienced – it is a Holy thing! Trust me; I have you right where you need to be to give birth to what I promised. Don't think for one minute that you are not ready for the assignment. Before you were ever formed in your mother's womb, I set you apart for this day. Now the day, the time, the moment has come. For there shall no more be a shadow of things to come, for thy light has come and the glory of the Lord is risen upon thee. The tangible hour of my glory has come, yet not without divine instructions, saith the Lord.*

In the natural, **Early Labor** consists of the onset of contractions at regular intervals. The contractions which feel like a painful and uncomfortable stretching for a matter of seconds, causes the woman's cervix to progressively dilate and efface. These contractions also cause the baby to descend ("drop"), making its way to the next phase of delivery. One would probably ask, "How this natural analogy is divinely connected to the Body of Christ?" There are many of you who have experienced hurt after hurt, set back after set back, and it seems as if you are heading in a descending direction instead of moving toward the promise. Let me provide you with clear revelation. If you feel as if what God has promised you is moving in the opposite direction, fear not. A downward spiral in areas of your life that you thought should be moving upward is a clear sign that the promise is making its way to the next phase of the birthing process.

The scripture says in II Corinthians 4:17-18, *"For our light affliction, which is but for a moment, worketh for us a far more exceeding and eternal weight of glory. While we look not at the things which are seen, but at the things which are not seen: for the things which are seen are temporal; but the things which are not seen are eternal."* You may be experiencing pain, delay and the very appearance of the promise seems so far off based on what you see right now. However, the Word of God says in I John 3:2, *"Beloved, now are we the sons of God, and it doth not yet appear what we shall be: but we know that, when he shall appear, we shall be like him; for we shall see him as he is."* You may not look like you are even pregnant with the promise, let alone in labor. But God is speaking to you today and He is making it clear and plain: **"You are on the verge of giving birth. Don't focus on what you feel like, what it looks like, neither what they said."** It is time for the believer to know that because you were born again; birthing will always be a part of your human existence on earth.

There is power in reproduction. This is why the enemy went after Adam and Eve in the garden. He knew then, as he knows now, we have the power to carry the seed as a partaker of the redemptive power of Jesus Christ. The Holy Spirit has the power to raise the seed up and cause the believer to give birth to that which has been planted. Yet, you are becoming frustrated right now because the enemy of your soul is throwing out distress calls with your bills, your family members, your job, and all else. Hear the Word of the Lord. The enemy only utilizes these earthly things to choke the Word, the seed that has been planted in you, out of you. Resist him right now and I assure you that he will flee from you. You are experiencing one problem after the other simply because you are one moment closer to giving birth to that in which God has promised.

When the contractions become closer and closer the doctor or midwife does an internal exam on the woman to determine her progress. Are you hearing me with your spiritual ear? Normally, the woman has progressed to *Active Labor* and the doctor/midwife does an internal exam *during a contraction* to determine the position and presentation of the baby. Most of the Body of Christ have gone through a purging process, where those things that were not like God had to be removed prior to entering into the birthing process. When you are carrying a baby in the natural, your will has to die that the seed may live. The same applies in the realm of the Spirit. The promise will live and not die and declare the works of the living God, only if you allow the flesh to be put to death.

Unlike *Early Labor,* during *Active Labor,* a woman is

normally not able to talk through labor contractions. The contractions become stronger and maybe intolerable. What am I saying? If you are not able to explain where you are in God right now, if you don't understand why you have been fasting, praying, believing, confessing, declaring and all else, yet nothing has happened, no visible sign of the promise, you like many others are speechless. God will allow you to be in a place where you can't feel Him or hear from Him. As a matter of fact, there seems to be no more conversation about what He promised. **RED ALERT TO EVERY BELIEVER READING THIS** – This is the time when God is doing His best work, when everything around you is silent.

In Psalms 22:1-3, in the New Living translation, the scripture says, *"My God, my God! Why have you forsaken me? Why do you remain so distant? Why do you ignore my cries for help? Every day I call to you, my God, but you do not answer. Every night you hear my voice, but I find no relief. Yet you are holy. The praises of Israel surround your throne."* He is a holy God, one who is revered and worthy of honor and worship. He will not bring dishonor or shame to His name by not bringing to pass what He has spoken. He is faithful to watch over His Word to perform it. In Psalm 89:33-34 in the New Living translation, the scripture says, *"But I will never stop loving him, nor let my promise to him fail. No, I will not break my covenant; I will not take back a single word I said."* God will not take back one word. He is a God of performance.

Although labors vary from woman to woman, there are certain coping techniques that are suggested during this phase of labor to assist the woman through this somewhat difficult time. One can utilize breathing exercises, relaxation techniques, massage and even gentle encouragement to help them cope. What am I saying to you? This is the time when you and I as believers must continue to breathe upon our promise by decreeing the Word that God spoke from the beginning that it may live (Ezekiel 37:9). You must also relax, cast your burdens on the Lord and He will sustain you (Psalm 55:22).

A massage in the natural is very similar to meditating on the Word day and night that your way may be made prosperous and you may obtain good success (Joshua 1:8). The massage removes toxins from the inward parts of your body. The same with the Word of God, as you meditate on it, receive its instruction and digest it, it will remove everything that is not like Him. When you and I continue to focus on the Word and not the pain, God will make our way prosperous and bring us into our destined success. Let me help you, if you are standing in agreement on a specific promise for someone, call them, write them and let them know that God has not forgotten and He will bring to pass what they have requested. You are a responsible member of the Body of Christ. Therefore, you must help the other part of your body by encouraging them to stand on the promises of God. Ask the Holy Spirit to assist you in being sensitive to the needs of the people at this time. Many are on the verge of giving up, but if you are sensitive and have an ear to hear, the Spirit of the living God will lead you to pray for them or call them in their time of need.

This is a painful and uncomfortable phase in the birthing process because the contractions will not cease until the baby has made his/her way out of the birth canal. It may be painful because although you can feel pain, you can't see what is causing the pain. This is that in which the prophets spoke of. It is the birthing of a strong nation and a great promise.

Doctors/midwives do however offer medications to relieve some of the pain and the pressure. But I was instructed by my doctor that you don't want to relieve too much pressure because it could hinder your ability to push in Stage 2. What am I saying right there? Don't curse where you are, you have been positioned for such a time as this to move to the next phase of delivery. It is time to move from glory to glory. You are being transitioned from where you are into the wealthy place that God has promised.

The *Transitioning* phase of the birthing process is the last part of the *Active* phase. It is called the transition period because it marks the transition to the second stage of labor, which is Pushing. This is the most intense part of labor. Contractions are usually very strong, coming about every two in a half to three minutes and lasting a minute or more. Some women find themselves shaking or even shivering during this time. Yet, the woman knows she has an assignment and cannot turn back now. During this phase the baby should have already descended (dropped), rotated (turned face down) and now probably crowned (the head may be visible). I'm going somewhere with this, hold on. I have two things to say to you. First, God has already turned this thing for your good. HE CANNOT LIE!

In the book of Numbers 23:19, in the New Living translation, the scripture says, *"God is not a man, that he should lie. He is not a human, that he should change his mind....I received a command to bless; he has blessed, and I cannot reverse it."* What the enemy meant for your bad, your faithful God has already turned it and made it good. Stop worrying! Don't be stressed, it could cause complications during delivery. Secondly, because you are in the season appointed by God, you will not be disappointed. This promise was not due to come last year, nor the year before, it was never meant to be premature, it was meant to come forth in this time, at this moment that the glory of the Lord could be revealed and all flesh (everyone that said it couldn't be done) would see it.

In closing the *Transitioning* phase could last from a few minutes to a few hours. However, though it may be the most intense, your level of anticipation increases. Because you know that you are but a short time of giving birth to the promise. I can't tell you what phase you are in right now, but the Holy Spirit will by the time you have read all of the stages. In Stage 2, you will realize that you can't push any way you want to during delivery. You could harm the baby/promise. Yet the doctor/midwife gives you explicit instructions on when to push and how. The pushing takes place during the time of the most intense contraction. I know your Spirit man caught that one. Upon reading the next stage, you will be convinced that Pushing is required to give birth to everything that God has promised you.

Chapter 17: Stage 2 – Pushing

"The Birthing Process Continues - Stage 2 - Pushing"

As the birthing process continues, I'm sure by now the contractions and the pain have intensified. Am I right? Of course I am. It is simply because you have reached the point of no return. You have pressed through **_"Stage 1- Early Labor, Active Labor and Transitioning",_** and now you have reached the next level in the birthing process.

In the natural, there are many questions that go through a woman's mind. For the believer reading this today, you too have the same questions during this stage of the birthing process. You would ask: "How can I get through this stage without causing harm to the baby/promise? How can I endure the pain, listen to the instructions of the midwife/doctor and yield the results that I have been promised all at the same time? How much longer is this going to take? It seems like I have been in labor for quite some time, yet the baby/promise is not here yet. I've given birth before, yet this one seems to be much more difficult than any of the other births. Why? I thought I would have this baby/promise in my arms by now?" Does any of this sound familiar? Sure it does. Okay, good, I am glad you had the opportunity to release your thoughts.

Now is the time to take a deep breath and relax in between

contractions. Depending upon what you are about to give birth to, it may be extremely painful, emotionally tiring and for some of you even time consuming. However, each will give birth in his/her appointed time. Therefore, death is imminent for the believer during this phase, because this is the stage where faith is required and flesh must be crucified. If you don't allow your flesh to die, you could risk harming the baby/promise in this stage. You have waited this long, why not press on a little bit further and offer up no resistance. Just go ahead and die to your way of doing things that the promise within you may live.

During ***Stage 2- Pushing***, it is routine for most midwives/doctors to coach the women to push with each contraction in an effort to speed up the baby's descent. In laymen's terms, when the pain is at its peak, the midwife/doctor instructs the woman to bear down and push through the pain, and push pass the unknown. What is God saying to the believer right here? Pushing requires faith. It is because most are pushing toward a goal, promise, a baby, a vision, yet the push will require an act of faith due to the circumstances at hand. Although it may be painful, you are pushing toward something that you cannot see. You are pushing toward an expected end that God has promised. You are hoping that what God spoke will be birthed out during this stage. I call it pushing by faith. The scripture says in Hebrews 11:1 in the

King James Version, *"Now faith is the substance of things hoped for, the evidence of things not seen."* The same verse in the New Living translation says, *"What is faith? It is the confident assurance that what we hope for is going to happen. It is the evidence of things we cannot yet see."*

Pushing requires a NOW FAITH. You don't have time to decide whether or not this is the right time or the right season. You are in your season of fulfillment and you must PUSH by faith. Unfortunately, you will not have everything you need and the circumstances may not be the best for you to have this baby/promise. However, your surrounding condition does not govern the time of the release, nor is it an indication that God will not perform as promised. Jesus was born in a manger to a virgin named Mary. Yes, it appeared to be the wrong time. Yet, it was supernaturally ordained of God. Therefore, you cannot look at your circumstance or your current situation. NOW is the acceptable year of our Lord and the fullness of time has come. Stop questioning whether or not this is the right time. The Word of the Lord for you from this portion of the book is NOW FAITH IS! Your NOW FAITH will be instrumental in producing the harvest that God has promised you.

As I mentioned earlier, there are so many things that go through a woman's mind during this stage. One of the most strenuous is, *"Will the baby/promise be healthy and look just like the ultrasound pictures have depicted?"* I must stop right here and tell you YES IT WILL! Remember, earlier when I told you about our second baby, Amariah? The doctors thought they saw some deficiency in Amariah's natural make-up. But our God prevailed. During that entire process, God reminded me of the scripture in the book of Habakkuk 2:3. The scripture says, *"For the vision is yet for an appointed time, but at the end it shall speak, and not lie: though it tarry, wait for it; because it will surely come, it will not tarry. Behold, his soul which is lifted up is not upright in him: but the just shall live by his faith."* God is speaking to you loud and clear. You don't need to be concerned whether or not the baby/promise will be premature, be born with deficiencies, if every body part will be in the right place or if it will pass a clean bill of health. Since this is the fullness of time, the baby/promise shall speak and not lie. It shall turn out just the way God spoke it.

In the book of Isaiah 55:11, the Word of the Lord says, *"So shall my word be that goeth forth out of my mouth: it shall not return unto me void, but it shall accomplish that which I please, and it shall prosper in the thing whereto I sent it."* What God spoke will be accomplished in your life. The words that He speaks they are spirit and they are life. God will not alter what He has spoken. He cannot lie. He will bring it to pass.

The scripture says in the book of Ezekiel 12:25, 28 in the Amplified Bible, *"For I am the Lord; I will speak, and the word that I shall speak shall be performed (come to pass); it shall be no more delayed or prolonged, for in your days, O rebellious house, I will speak the word and will perform it, says the Lord God.....There shall none of My words be deferred any more, but the word which I have spoken shall be performed, says the Lord God."* Your days of delay and waiting have come to an end. However, faith without works is dead. Now is the time to apply faith to your works.

You have stayed the course in spite of the many obstacles you have faced with the birth of this promise. You're almost there. Just stay focused and know that in which you have carried in your spirit is soon to become a tangible manifestation. Yet, there is one more significant thing you must do during this stage to see it. You must PUSH pass doubt, fear, the naysayers, hurt, disappointment, resentment, and a painful past. Despite these many stumbling blocks, you and the rest of the kingdom of heaven knows that you must give birth.

This is not an assignment that can be passed on to someone else. You must give birth to it and move to the next level that God has ordained for you, your family, your ministry, your professional career and all others that are connected to your birthing process.

You must remember, **there will always be something that you must PUSH pass to give birth to that in which God has placed in your spirit**. However, if you have been in total alignment with God, the pain is a sure indication that the promise is near. Therefore, *Pushing* is inevitable; it cannot be avoided. Just remember, the pain is a prerequisite for the PUSH!

In closing, we discussed in an earlier chapter that the book of Micah, Chapter 4 says that you will be in pain to bring forth. You have pain only to bring forth what God has purposed for your life as a believer. I want to rid each of you of the false hope that you will not experience pain on your journey to fulfillment in the kingdom of God. It may be in the most confusing place; at the most difficult time in your life, yet the pain cannot be avoided. However, *Pushing* pass the pain is mandatory to see what it is behind the pain.

If you are in pain today, God is trying to reveal something to you. It can only be exposed if you PUSH! Some of you would ask, with what and how? The acronym P.U.S.H. stands for several instructional tactics for the believer to use in the midst of pain. 1) Praise Until Something Happens - Psalm 8:2, Praise ceases the plans of the enemy. You must open up your mouth and praise God in spite of what it looks or feels like. 2) Pray Until Something Happens - I Thessalonians 5:17, Pray without ceasing.

You must continue in prayer that you may be strengthened in your inner man. 3) Prophecy Until Something Happens - Job 22:28, *"Thou shalt also decree a thing, and it shall be established unto thee."* Open up your mouth and decree what God has already said, that it may be established. 4) Pursue Until Something Happens - Isaiah 26:9, *"With my soul have I desired thee in the night; yea, with my spirit within me will I seek thee early."* You must come after God with your whole heart. The scripture also says in the book of Matthew 7:7, *"...Seek and you shall find."* You must seek God to find the treasure within your earthen vessel. 5) Persevere Until Something Happens - Romans 8:38, *"For I am persuaded, that neither death, nor life, nor angels, nor principalities, nor powers, nor things present, nor things to come...shall be able to separate us from the love of God, which is Christ Jesus our Lord."* You must not allow any circumstance, person, or anything separate you from God; you must persevere. This means you must continue in your efforts in the kingdom. You must keep moving until something happens and until you have given birth to all that God has promised you - P.U.S.H.!

In the book of John 16:21 the scripture says, *"A woman when she is in travail hath sorrow, because her hour is come: but as soon as she is delivered of the child, she remembereth no more the anguish, for joy that a man is born into the world."* Once you have given birth to that in which God has promised you, you will forget the pain that it caused you. It will be a memory. Focus on the end and on what God has spoken. As well as, all God has showed you. Now is not the time to give up. You have reached the point of no return! All of those who are needed to assist you in this delivery are in the right place. Today, you have received your instructions from the Holy Spirit, who is the voice that goes beyond reason and the Spirit without measure. Listen carefully once again. **During the most intense pain, and the most difficult time in your life, you must PUSH to yield the results that God has promised.**

Chapter 18: Stage 3 – Delivering of the Placenta

"The Birthing Process - Stage 3 – Delivering of the Placenta"

In the last chapter you read about ***"The Birthing Process – Stage 2 – Pushing."*** Therefore, if you were in that stage, by now, you are totally exhausted. You now have a tangible manifestation of the promise in which you carried from the time the seed was planted. Contrary to popular belief, the promise came forth with nothing less than what God had spoken. As a matter of fact, it exceeded your expectation. The Word of God says in Ephesians 3:20, *"Now unto him that is able to do exceeding abundantly above all that we ask or think, according to the power that worketh in us."* No matter what you are believing God for, you must not accept anything less than exceeding. Why? Because exceeding is where God starts; it is His barometer.

In Stage 2, you PUSHED pass pain, pressure, shame, disappointment, fear, and all else to give birth to the promise. However, there is one more PUSH required. The misconception about giving birth is once the baby/promise is delivered, many believe the worst is over. This is partially true. In the birthing process there are three stages, the last stage is ***"Delivering the Placenta."*** In laymen's terms, when the fetus (baby/promise) is delivered, the placenta is delivered afterwards; that is why it is often called the ***after birth***. Please hear me this morning with your spiritual ear. This is a very important part of the birthing process. However, many don't discuss this process because the delivery thereof is not as painful. Yet, if it is not removed, deadly repercussions could follow. Read this next statement very slowly: **The birthing process is not over until the *after birth* has been delivered.**

The medical definition for *placenta* is described as the tissue that is created to connect the mother and the fetus. During pregnancy, the placenta transports nourishment and removes waste. In my studies, I discovered that under normal circumstances, the mother's blood does not flow directly into the baby, nor does the baby's blood enter the mother's bloodstream. Among the many tasks performed by the placenta, it serves as a blood filter, keeping the mother's blood on one side and the baby on the other side. It is my understanding that toxins and other substances can pass through the membrane. Therefore, doctors encourage mothers to be very careful of what they ingest and breathe in. Don't get lost in the medical definition, here is the spiritual revelation. In the natural, the placenta is the tissue that connects the mother and the fetus. In the spirit, the Word of God is what connects you to your unborn promise.

The scripture says in John 1:1-4, *"In the beginning was the*

Word, and the Word was with God, and the Word was God. All things were made by him; and without him was not any thing made that was made. In him was life; and the life was the light of men." Therefore, neither you nor the promise can survive without being connected to each other by the Word of God. The Word is a seed, when it is planted it must be nourished by the Word. I hope you read the last statement with understanding. When God gives you a promise, whether it is a promise for healing, prosperity, household salvation and anything else, it cannot survive alone. The Word must receive the Word in order for it to grow into the full grown harvest that has been predestined. However, if it does not receive the proper nourishment, it will become malnourished and die. Why? The placenta is connected to the fetus by the umbilical cord. The umbilical cord is what the baby/promise must remain connected to until birth. I believe the believer's umbilical cord is described as "the vine" in the book of John.

The scripture says in John 15:4-5, in the New Living Translation, *"Remain in me, and I will remain in you. For a branch cannot produce fruit if it is severed from the vine, and you cannot be fruitful apart from me. Yes, I am the vine; you are the branches. Those who remain in me, and I in them, will produce much fruit. For apart from me you can do nothing."* The scripture says in Proverbs 4:7, *"Wisdom is the principal thing; therefore get wisdom: and with all thy getting get understanding."* I have understanding now. I understand why some of us never see our promises manifested. It is very simple: we disconnect from the vine because we either get tired of waiting or get tired of trying to see by the flesh instead of walking by faith and not by sight. We faint too quickly. We throw in the towel when we receive a bad report, instead of pressing toward the mark for the prize that was prophesied. Okay, the time for that is over.

You can no longer think because it hasn't come, it is not coming. Delayed does not mean denied. Delayed could mean several things. One of those things being, maybe it isn't time for the promise to be birthed. God does not specialize in premature babies. In the natural, premature babies require further nurturing outside of the womb. However, spiritually, God desires for what you carry as a believer to be hidden until the fullness of time comes.

For those of you, who say you are ready to step out on faith to do what God has instructed, don't miss ALL of what God is speaking about your assignment. If He tells you to do research, follow instructions. If He tells you to sit down and talk to people who are doing what you desire to do, follow the instructions. There are so many people depending on your obedience in this season – FOLLOW ALL THE INSTRUCTIONS – DON'T TAKE

ANY SHORTCUTS! If you move before your time in the field, the assignment or the promise could risk not receiving its proper intake of oxygen for survival. Even for those of you reading this that have businesses and ministries; it is wise to not begin any new projects without the complete guidance and direction of the Holy Spirit. This could result in you giving birth to a premature promise. I realized some of us move too slow and the other half of us move too fast. This is the Word of the Lord for you today – WAIT FOR COMPLETE INSTRUCTIONS!

I must digress for a moment and give you something the Spirit of the Living God gave to me many years ago. In the book of Joshua, Chapter 3, Joshua and the children of Israel were preparing to cross over the Jordan River. However, they were a bit concerned because they had not traveled to this new place before and were like some of us, unsure of the outcome. Does this sound familiar? As they proceeded to walk in faith, Joshua was receiving instructions from the Lord and passing the instructions on to the children of Israel. But one of the most profound revelations I received after reading Joshua 3:1-8, was in verse 8. The scripture says in Joshua 3:8 in the New Living Translation, *"Give these instructions to the priests who are carrying the Ark of the Covenant: When you reach the banks of the Jordan River, take a few steps into the river and stop."* For those of you who are Bible scholars, there are four sources that come together to form the Jordan River, which most of us call the promise land. They all arise at the foothills of Mount Hermon. **The Jordan River flows through <u>3 stages</u> before it reaches its final destination – the end of the promise.** Sometimes, the Body of Christ is in such a hurry to reach the promise land that we fail to follow explicit instructions while on our journey.

In the above mentioned scripture (Joshua 3:8), the Lord instructed the priests to take a few steps into the river and stop. What was He saying? It was very simple. He instructed them to take a few steps at a time and stop. He was teaching them how to follow the instructions one step at a time. What point am I making? Don't be in such a hurry to get to the promise land and then when you get there you don't know what to do or how to handle what is in the land. As believers, we must be quick to hear the voice of God, obey and wait for further instructions. Don't allow people to place you in positions when you know it is not what God has spoken. There is a time and a season for all things. You don't want to give birth in the wrong season and risk having a premature baby/promise. The scripture says in Psalm 27:14, *"Wait on the Lord: be of good courage, and he shall strengthen thine heart: wait, I say, on the Lord."* Don't be afraid to wait! The fullness of the promise is depending on you to follow instructions.

I pray you have an understanding. Although I had not planned to include any of this in this part of the book, I have learned to follow instructions, because my obedience is connected to someone else's harvest.

Now before I close this chapter, I want to complete this stage of ***"Delivering the Placenta."*** As I mentioned earlier, the placenta also removes wastes and serves as a blood filter. In its function as a blood filter, it separates the mother's blood, as well as the baby's; **the two never meet**. In the book of Hebrews 4:12, the scripture says, *"For the word of God is quick, and powerful and sharper than any twoedged sword, piercing even to the dividing asunder of soul and spirit, and of the joints and marrow, and is a discerner of the thoughts and intents of the heart."* You must continue to let the Word of the Lord remove anything that would hinder the growth and development of the promise. You must separate yourself from all those things that can be harmful to you and the unborn promise in this season. You cannot afford to miss what rightfully belongs to you. You cannot ingest anything that will not digest in your spirit man. In essence, you can no longer separate yourself from what provides and nurtures the very existence of what you carry – the Word of God.

As the doctor/midwife proceeds to assist the woman in the delivery of the placenta, he/she may ask her to PUSH one last time.

Upon its exit, the placenta is checked by the doctor/midwife to make sure that all things were removed from within its circumference shape and delivered successfully. However, I want you to understand this principal. Once the promise is delivered, you still have divine responsibilities **after** its **birth.** Don't think for one minute that you are finished PUSHING, finished declaring the Word of God, and you can now move on to something else because NOW IT IS TIME FOR YOU TO HANDLE WHAT COMES **after** the **birth! After** the **birth,** you must continue to maintain your relationship with the true vine – Jesus; for without Him you can do nothing. There will be another birth and another birth and another birth. We are a people who were born again to give birth again and again. However, the only way a believer can experience a life of continuous birthing, is if he/she remains connected to the giver of life, Jesus.

God does not want the believer to become comfortable in this season. Becoming comfortable will be a type of birth control pill that can postpone your ability to become spiritually pregnant once again. Don't become comfortable with just receiving your healing. Begin telling others how they too can be healed. Lay hands on the sick and watch them recover. Don't become comfortable because all of your family members are saved; help someone who desires to see that same thing happen in their family.

Don't become comfortable because the one business idea God gave you is prospering, go after the prize – there is much more for you than one business. What am I saying? Don't become comfortable because you have given birth to one promise, because there is much more to come **after** the **birth!** But you must remain connected to the God of all birthing – Jesus Christ. He is the author and finisher of your faith. Once He plants a seed, He will see it through until the end. However, you must remain connected to Him to see the end of all that He has promised you. If you want to experience life and that more abundantly **after** the **birth** of one promise, remain in His presence where there is fullness of joy and a life of no limits.

Chapter 19: "Giving Birth to a Breech Nation"

"Giving Birth to a Breech Nation"

In this chapter of The Birthing Process I want to talk to you about something that is very close and dear to my heart. I have become gravely concerned over the past several years about what I am seeing and hearing in the Body of Christ as I travel around the world. It is something that must be addressed so that we can be redirected as to what God's heart is regarding such and the pattern He desires for us to follow in the spiritual birthing process and how covenant relationships are vital in this process.

First, let me say this there can be no spiritual conception without an intimate, blood covenant relationship with the Lord Jesus Christ. You must be married to this Word to carry its baby. You cannot be in today and out tomorrow. You cannot love God today and not like your neighbor tomorrow. You must be married to this Word without thinking about divorce; so that you can effectively carry the semen of this Word that will produce results and allow you to birth fruit in its right season every time.

There are no premature births in God. The scripture says in II Peter 1:3-8, *"According as his divine power hath given unto us all things that pertain unto life and godliness, through the knowledge of him that hat called us to glory and virtue: Whereby are given unto us exceeding great and precious promises: that by these ye might be partakers of the divine nature, having escaped the corruption that is in the world through lust. And beside this, giving all diligence, add to your faith virtue; and to virtue knowledge; And to knowledge temperance; and to temperance patience; and to patience godliness; And to godliness brotherly kindness; and to brotherly kindness charity. For if these things be in you, and abound, they make you that ye shall neither be barren nor unfruitful in the knowledge of our Lord Jesus Christ. But he that lacketh these things is blind, and cannot see afar off, and hath forgotten that he was purged from his old sins. Wherefore the rather, brethren, give diligence to make your calling and election sure: for if ye do these things, ye shall never fall."* This scripture tells us if you are housing, eating, and communing daily with that which pertains to godliness then you will never be barren or unfruitful because this Word always births forth results. However, despite what I know to be the truth in the Word of God, I am noticing many breeched babies are being birthed in the kingdom of God. Many would ask, "What is a *breeched birth*?" In the natural, a *breech birth* is the birth of a baby from a breech presentation. In the breech presentation the baby normally enters the birth canal with the buttocks or feet first as opposed to the normal head first presentation. I discovered that there are many factors that can encourage breeched presentation. However, prematurity is likely the chief cause. When the labor is premature the incidence of breech presentation is higher.

There are many dangers in breeched births. One in particular is oxygen deprivation that occurs because of the direction in which the baby is turned. As well as, the prolonged compression of the umbilical cord during birth. All of this is manifested because of head entrapment. If oxygen deprivation is prolonged it could cause neurological damage or even death in some instances. Most breeched births are delivered by C-section if the woman has not reached full term. As a matter of fact, statistics show that 25 percent of babies are in the breeched position at 32 weeks gestation. However, there are times when the baby can be turned around within the woman by the midwife or doctor before the onset of labor. Either way, there are risks involved because of the abnormal direction of the baby.

Furthermore, in most cases where twins are in the womb, it is highly likely for the first twin to exit head first, but the second to be in a breeched position and must be repositioned for survival. How is this directly related to the Body of Christ and where we are now as a people? A spiritually breeched birth is anything that enters the birth canal before its time in the field. It is that which is considered unripe. It is that which is birthed in power, yet does not possess the head knowledge and the wisdom required to carry that power with grace, love and humility. You cannot desire the power of God, yet reject His wisdom. You are a walking endangered species in the earth with no desire to receive or walk with God's instructions.

I believe that the full implementation of the book of Titus, Chapter 2, is vital to the growth of believers today. The scripture say in Titus:3-5, *"The aged women likewise that they be in behaviour as becometh holiness, not false accusers, not given to much wine, teachers of good things; That they may teach the young women to be sober, to love their husbands, to love their children, to be discreet, chaste, keepers at home, good, obedient to their own husbands, that the word of God be not blasphemed."* This scripture tells us that it is our responsibility as the older women to teach the younger. Older does not always dictate age. Older may be in experience. However, I believe we are in a season that we must teach the younger how to birth out what God spoke to them with wisdom, knowledge and understanding from on high. We must teach them how to birth it out in its right season. We must teach young men and women how desiring the next platform was not the goal of Jesus Christ, but desiring the sincere milk of His Word and His wisdom.

God's desire in the birthing process is for all things to be birthed head first. What does that mean? The scripture says in II

Chronicles 1:9-12, *"Now, O Lord God, let thy promise unto David my father be established: for thou hast made me king over a people like the dust of the earth in multitude. Give me now wisdom and knowledge, that I may go out and come in before this people: for who can judge this thy people, that is so great? And God said to Solomon, Because this was in thine heart, and thou hast not asked for riches, wealth, or honour, nor the life of thine enemies, neither yet hast asked long life; but hast asked wisdom and knowledge for thyself, that thou mayest judge my people, over whom I have made thee king: Wisdom and knowledge is granted unto thee; and I will give thee riches, and wealth, and honour, such as none of the kings have had that have been before thee, neither shall there any after thee have the life."* It is time to teach our sons and daughters, and the rest of the Body of Christ that it's not the power that they need to seek. It's not the fame; it's not the riches; and it's not whose bag you are holding that you need to be in pursuit of. None of that means anything if you don't seek the wisdom and knowledge of God!

The scripture says in James 1:5, *"If any of you lack wisdom, let him ask of God, that giveth to all men liberally, and upbraideth not; and it shall be given him."* Honestly, I don't want the power if I don't have the wisdom of God required so that I can know how to use it. We have loose cannons in the Body of Christ right now because many have given birth to a breeched baby and the baby is still deprived of oxygen. This is the spiritual oxygen that comes to everything you give birth to that it may live and not die and declare the works of the living God.

There is a wisdom that comes with being birthed in the way God intended – head first. The scripture says in Matthew 6:33, *"But seek ye first the kingdom of God and its righteousness and all these things will be added unto you."* If you follow the pattern of the kingdom of God and seek God first, He will give you the power, anointing, and all that you need that pertains to life and godliness. Man cannot do that for you.

Too many times people believe that if you are the one who holds the leader's bible, carry their luggage or minister to them in whatever capacity; this automatically makes you a candidate for the anointing and the wisdom of God. Well I have an announcement for you: ABSOLUTELY NOT! You must seek God first, just like they had to seek Him first. The anointing is not going to roll off their bible, off their shirt or whatever the case may be and be transferred on to you. As leaders we must teach the younger that they must pursue God to get His wisdom. Staying connected to a leader will provide an impartation, but a believer can only get pregnant in the presence of God!

We have sons and daughters in the faith perishing because

of lack of knowledge. They are seeking the power, and rejecting the wisdom of God. It is your assignment and mine as leaders to teach the younger that wisdom is the principal thing. The scripture says in Proverbs 4:7, *"Wisdom is the principal thing; therefore get wisdom: and with all thy getting get understanding."* The scripture says that wisdom is the principal thing. This speaks volumes to me because without it you lack understanding. Without wisdom, you will not only hurt others, but you will corrupt a nation that is to be birthed out of your loins.

The scripture says in Proverbs 8:11, *"For wisdom is better than rubies; and all the things that may be desired are not to be compared to it."* Today, God wants us to incline our ear to wisdom and apply our hearts to understanding. According to Proverbs 2:6, it is the Lord that gives wisdom and we must pursue it. The scripture says in Job 28:12-23, *"But where shall wisdom be found? and where is the place of understanding? Man knoweth not the price thereof; neither is it found in the land of the living. The depth saith, It is not in me: and the sea saith, It is not with me. It cannot be gotten for gold, neither shall silver be weighed for the price thereof. It cannot be valued with the gold of Ophir, with the precious onyx, or the sapphire. The gold and the crystal cannot equal it: and the exchange of it shall not be for jewels of fine gold. No mention shall be made of coral, or of pearls: for the price of wisdom is above rubies. The topaz of Ethiopia shall not equal it, neither shall it be valued with pure gold. Whence then cometh wisdom? and where is the place of understanding? Seeing it is hid from the eyes of all living, and kept close from the fowls of the air. Destruction and death say, We have heard the fame thereof with our ears. God understandeth the way thereof, and he knoweth the place thereof."* If God understands the way of wisdom and knows the place of it, you must seek Him to get it. There is a natural wisdom that comes with age and experience that you gain on your journey through this age and time. However, if you desire to know the mysteries of God, you must pursue Him and acknowledge Him in all your ways to get it.

The scripture says in Psalm 51:5-6, *"Behold, I was shapen in iniquity; and in sin did my mother conceive me. Behold, thou desirest truth in the inward parts: and in the hidden part thou shalt make me to know wisdom."* This should be your prayer and mine, "Lord I desire to carry truth in my inward parts. Make me to know your wisdom in the hidden part that I may not give birth to a breeched nation."

There are many other scriptures about wisdom. The scripture says in Job 28:28, *"....the fear of the Lord, that is wisdom..."* Then the scripture says in Psalm 111:10, *"The fear of the Lord is the beginning of wisdom."* I honestly believe that as scary as this sounds there is a loss of fear in the Body of Christ. People do not have the fear of God because they have become too common with God. Let me make something prophetically clear: You are not that smart. You need His wisdom. The scripture says in Proverbs 2:7 that wisdom is laid up for the righteous. Therefore, all you and I have to do is pursue it. However, I discovered this truth that people resist pursuing His wisdom because it will expose their insufficiencies and expose the true thoughts and intents in their heart. But according to Proverbs, Chapter 4, you cannot build what God desires for you to have without His wisdom. Thus, if you are building a home, business, ministry or anything in God, it will not stand without His wisdom.

In the book of Genesis, Chapter 25, we find the birth of twins, Jacob and Esau. These twins in the womb in Genesis 25:21-26 exemplified a power struggle from within that did not end even after the exit. The scripture says in the book of Genesis 25:21-26, *"And Isaac intreated the Lord for his wife, because she was barren: and the Lord was intreated of him, and Rebekah his wife conceived. And the children struggled together within her; and she said, If it be so, why am I thus? And she went to enquire of the Lord. And the Lord said unto her, Two nations are in thy womb, and two manner of people shall be separated from thy bowels; and the one people shall be stronger than the other people; and the elder shall serve the younger. And when her days to be delivered were fulfilled, behold, there were twins in her womb. And the first came out red, all over like an hairy garment; and they called his name Esau. And after that came his brother out, and his hand took hold on Esau's heel; and his name was called Jacob: and Isaac was threescore years old when she bare them."* Rebekah, Isaac's wife, was barren. After 20 years, Isaac prayed and Rebekah conceives. Rebekah felt an inner struggle and inquired of the Lord why there appeared to be a war taking place within her. The Lord of course gives her an answer and tells her that there are two nations in her womb, which were two different kinds of people. In essence, Rebekah was carrying twins.

We can look at the twins as being one of the spirit and one of the flesh. This spoke volumes to me. After reading the scriptures repetitively, I came to many conclusions that startled me. I realized that it is possible for someone to give birth to a ministry in the flesh, and a business in the flesh. People do it every day without the sovereign guidance of God. Unfortunately, they birth it based upon their own wisdom, understanding, and personal merit, professional and educational degrees. I am simply saying that you can give birth in the flesh to anything you want versus the thing that God spoke. This is what I consider breech because you did not provide it with its proper eternal oxygen for it to be sustained.

Let me interject something here. In the book of Isaiah 33:6, the scripture says, *"And wisdom and knowledge shall be the stability of thy times, and strength of salvation: the fear of the Lord is his treasure."* Despite what many of us know and have possessed as natural wisdom, we need the kind of wisdom that will keep us stable in turbulent times....IT IS THE WISDOM OF GOD!

So Rebekah discovers these two nations in her womb; one would be stronger than the other and the elder would serve the younger. I want you to remember what was said earlier about twins. (The first normally comes out head first, but the second twin has a high possibility of being breeched.)

The first twin to exit Rebekah's womb was Esau. Esau's name means, rough, sensibly felt, handled, make or completely developed. This tells me that Esau was completely developed – nothing missing and nothing broken. Then the second twin, Jacob, who was the younger twin, makes his exit. The scripture in Genesis, Chapter 25, said that he took the heel of his brother Esau as he was exiting the birth canal. Jacob's name means, heel catcher, trickster, supplanter, leg-puller, he who follows the heel of one, one who deceives, circumvent and restrain. Esau was the completely developed one and Jacob who grabs a hold of Esau's heel as he is exiting the womb makes a strong implication to us as we are talking about giving birth to a breeched nation. If you are reading this and have been assigned as a leader in ministry – one of your assignments is to teach the younger. Hear me clearly by the Spirit. **If you exit the womb first, if you start your ministry first, or if God launches you first, don't let people deceive you and hold on to your heel for wisdom. You point them in the direction of the Lord where they can seek His wisdom and His way and not be deceived or tricked out of their inheritance!** I do not let people hold on to me like that because they will lose sight of what their feet can do.

The Lord told Joshua in Joshua, Chapter 1, Moses my servant, is dead. Where ever the sole of your foot tread that land I have given unto you to possess. Our assignment is to lead the younger into the presence of God so that when we are dead, or no longer even doing what God instructs us to do, they will not fall. In seeking the wisdom of God and not the wisdom of man, the Word of God will be imbedded in them and they will continue to follow the steps that have been ordered by God, not by their mentor or spiritual parent.

When you have people who look up to you and follow you, you must respond like Paul. In I Corinthians 11:1, Paul said, *"Be ye followers of me, even as I also am of Christ."* In essence, Paul told the people, follow me....BUT ONLY FOLLOW ME AS I FOLLOW CHRIST! You should not follow people because you want something out of it other than the wisdom that God will give you.

In being an example to others in the kingdom of God, many that you mentor will be like Ruth was to Naomi. They will do what you do. This is why you must live a life above reproach because if you don't go to church, they won't go to church. If you don't tithe, they won't tithe. If you don't show love towards your neighbor, they won't know how to show love.

What I am seeing in the Body of Christ is people saying do as I say but NOT AS I DO! It is what God considers a breeched birth. My assignment and yours is to make sure if we see any of these in the "body" we will immediately TURN IT AROUND WITH THE WISDOM OF GOD so they won't perish! When you understand the power and the wisdom that God possesses then you will have the power.

In Ecclesiasts 9:18, the scripture says, *"Wisdom is better than weapons of war..."* If you have the wisdom of God, you can obtain the strategies necessary to win every battle. What many leaders are teaching the younger is seek to be on the next platform, seek to be on television, seek to be rich through ministry, and seek to be in the company of the greatest prophets. But I want you to hear the Spirit of the Lord speaking to you loud and clear, when you are in the presence of the Lord, you are ALREADY IN THE COMPANY OF ONE OF THE GREATEST PROPHETS THAT EVER LIVED AND HE IS STIL LIVING! Though He died on a cross and was buried, He ever lives now making intercession for you and I.

Those other things are not what you should be seeking. The scripture says in Proverbs 23:4, *"Labour not to be rich and cease from your own wisdom."* This is not what you should be laboring for. In the book of Proverbs, Chapter 1, our safety is in seeking the wisdom of God, not the wisdom of man. Your fruitfulness will manifest from seeking the wisdom of God and not the wisdom of man. God desires for us as believers to seek wise counsel but not before we seek Him first! Remember, head **first** is the proper birthing position.

The scripture says in Colossians 1:18, *"And he is the head of the body, the church: who is the beginning, the firstborn from the dead; that in all things he might have the preeminence."* Jesus is the head of the body and you must seek His wisdom to get understanding. He is the love of God that does not bring you to the birth and then shuts the womb. If it came from Him and He is the Father of the conception, every conception will result in a full manifestation every time.

I thought about Ishmael while the Lord was giving me this chapter. Ishmael was born out of zeal, impatience, and lust not love. I thought about him because the love of God always brings forth fruit in its season. But what I have discovered is this, when in fact you are in Christ, every thing in Christ bears fruit. However, if you are not in the right field like Ruth was, you will miss your harvest. Too many times believers follow a move of God and not the will of God and miss the field. This lets me know that many are missing the syncopated choreographic move of God and focusing on the steps of man. So when the man moves or falls into disappointment, the person that is attached to him/her falls into the same level of disappointment or greater. Why? It is simply because they are attached to the move of man and not the move of God.

Any time you are attached to God, daily commune with Him and are divinely connected to the umbilical cord of His Word, the scripture says in John 15:2-5, *"Every branch in me that beareth not fruit he taketh away: and every branch that beareth fruit, he purgeth it, that it may bring forth more fruit. Now ye are clean through the word which I have spoken unto you. Abide in me, and I in you. As the branch cannot bear fruit of itself, except it abide in the vine; no more can ye, except ye abide in me. I am the vine, ye are the branches: He that abideth in me, and I in him, the same bringeth forth much fruit: for without me ye can do nothing."* Everything in God bears fruit and when it gets to a place that it's supposed to be bearing fruit and it's not, God begins a cutting process or a separating process. This is the same process that takes place in a breeched birth. A C-section is performed to provide an exit for the baby who is in danger because of its position or location within the womb.

In the book of Mark, Chapter 11, Jesus and the disciples are in Bethphage. Bethphage is the place or house of the unripe figs. Actually, chronologically, this event took place a week before his crucifixion. Jesus provides instructions to two unnamed disciples. He tells them to go into the village and as soon as they get there they would find a colt where no one has ever sat on him. He instructed them to bring the colt to Him and if anybody ask what for just tell them that He had need of the colt.

The scripture says in Mark 11:12-14, 20, *"And on the morrow, when they were come from Bethany, he was hungry: and seeing a fig tree afar off having leaves, he came, if haply he might find any thing thereon: and when he came to it, he found nothing but leaves; for the time of figs was not yet. And Jesus answered and said unto it, No man eat fruit of thee hereafter for ever. And his disciples heard it...And in the morning, as they passed by, they saw the fig tree dried up from the roots."* First, let's discuss the fig tree and why Jesus cursed it. You would have to know the characteristics of fig trees to understand why Jesus cursed the tree.

The fruit of the fig tree generally appears before the leaves and because the fruit is green it sort of blends in with the leaves right up until it is almost ripe. So when Jesus and His disciples saw from a distance that the tree had leaves, they would have expected it to also have fruit on it even though it was earlier in the season than what would be normal for a fig tree to be bearing fruit. Then from studying about the way fig trees grow in Israel, I learned that each tree would often produce two to three crops of figs each season. Seemingly, there would be an early crop in the spring, followed by one or two later crops. In some parts of the area, depending on climate and conditions, it was also possible that a tree might produce fruit 10 out of 12 months. This also explained to me why Jesus and His disciples would be looking for fruit on the fig tree even if it was not in the main growing season.

The fact that the tree already had leaves on it even though it was at a higher elevation around Jerusalem, and therefore would have been outside of the normal season for figs, would have seemed to be a good indication that there would also be fruit on it. Let me make something clear. The true lesson of the fig tree to leaders is that we should bear spiritual fruit according to Galatians 5:22-23 and not give an appearance of religiosity like the

Sadducees or the temple priests. When Jesus cursed the fig tree, He was basically denouncing unfruitful Christians. Those people who profess to be a Christian, have a love-relationship with God and claim to be carriers of His seed, yet they possess no evidence of that relationship. Any time you are carrying the Word of God there will be a SURE manifestation of what you are carrying. It will not be premature, immature, breeched or void of fullness.

The presence of a fruitful fig tree was considered to be a symbol of blessing and prosperity for the nation of Israel (Jeremiah 8:6-13). When you bear fruit spiritually, it is a clear indication that you have been blessed by God. The fruit that is birthed spiritually according to the book of Galatians, Chapter 5, begins with love. Then all these other things will be added unto you.

Chapter 20: "More About the Afterbirth"

"More About the Afterbirth "

As I press toward the end of this book, it is imperative that I remain in the birthing room with you until you have given birth to everything God promised. The Lord has given me an anointing to teach, minister and write from the aspect of spiritual intercourse, conception and delivery. This section of the book will be strategic in pressing you past the delivery of the baby or the promise right into what happens immediately after the baby is born. **It is more about the release of the afterbirth.** After I finished writing the last chapter, I realized that there was so much more that you needed to know. I have discovered the fear that most women have in the natural about giving birth is the not knowing what to expect. Therefore, just like the Word of God says in Hosea 4:6, men perish because of lack of knowledge. I believe the problem that we have as believers is not knowing or fully recognizing where we are in our spiritual birthing process. If we knew where we were in the spiritual birthing process, when we encounter certain situations we would know what we should be doing. Better yet, we could be proactive instead of reactive. Right now, I know exactly where I am. I am feeding one baby and by the time this book is released, I would have birthed three more. You must know in your spirit where you are so that you will not become frustrated with this thing called The Birthing Process.

Here is "more" about the afterbirth that will assist you in this journey called the birthing process. When the fetus is born, its placenta begins a physiological separation for spontaneous expulsion afterwards (and for this reason is often called the afterbirth). Among organs, it is unique. It is the only organ in the human body that serves a vital function and then becomes obsolete. It is humanity's only disposable organ. Although the afterbirth is much smaller and usually is not accompanied with pain, it is disk-shaped and at full term measures about seven inches. The number seven is God's perfect number. It is the number of completion.

When Jesus was at the place called Golgotha, which was known as the place of the skull in John, Chapter 19, He was already in a complete place to be delivered. The skull in a human's head has seven holes; which is connected to the neck that has seven bones. If you read John 19:36, the scripture tells us that none of His bones were broken. Why? Because although it was the place of His crucifixion and worst pain, it was the place predestined by God to finish the work that He had purposed. You need to tell yourself today, *"I am in the place where the work will be finished and Jesus will be glorified."*

The seven holes in the human skull and seven bones in the

human neck equal 14. The number 14 means complete deliverance and salvation for generations. Whether you realize it or not, in this season of the afterbirth, you are in your place of complete deliverance and salvation for generations will come. This is why those who have stiff necks and are operating against what God instructed you to do are not working against you. They are working against the complete and the finished work of Christ.

I must show you something I discovered in John 19:28-30. I reflected intently on the life of Jesus during this chapter. Upon giving it some serious thought, Jesus could have come down from the cross at any moment. However, He was trying to teach the Body of Christ a very valuable lesson about the endurance of your faith. You must hang in there until you have given birth to everything that is connected to the promise.

The scripture says in the book of John 19:26-28, *"When Jesus therefore saw his mother, and the disciple standing by, whom he loved, he saith unto his mother, Woman, behold thy son! Then saith he to the disciple, Behold thy mother! And from that hour that disciple took her unto his own home. After this, Jesus knowing that all things were now accomplished, that the scripture might be fulfilled, saith, I thirst."* I have a very creative imagination and after I finished reading these verses of scripture, I said, "Lord this sounds just like the presentation the doctor makes after the baby comes out of the womb." It sounds like this: *"Mrs. Howard here is your beautiful baby.....hello baby, here is your mommy....you recognize that voice...."* The doctor or the midwife makes an introduction one to the other of the mother and the child. This verse of scripture became alive to me when the disciple says, *"Behold thy mother!"* Then immediately after in verse 27, the scripture says, *"And from that hour..."* In every labor and delivery unit, the doctor has at least up to 1-2 hours to deliver the placenta, but most do it immediately after the birth. Then in verse 28, the scripture says, *"After this, Jesus knowing that all things were now accomplished, that the scripture might be fulfilled, saith, I thirst."* What point am I making? You had to endure the "hard thing" so that you can have an AFTER THIS experience. The clock is set at an appointed and you are right on schedule to have an AFTER THIS experience in God! Get ready man of God. Get ready woman of God because you are about to have an after the fact experience in God! The fact of the matter may be one thing, but you house the truth and you are about to have an AFTER THE FACT, and AFTER THIS experience in God!

The scripture says in the book of Revelation 4:1, *"After this I looked, and behold, a door was opened in heaven..."* There are doors that will be opened AFTER THIS! After the birth is an AFTER THIS experience that will launch you like a missile into the field of your desire. Don't faint, you are in a land called "AFTER THIS!" I pray you are hearing me by the Spirit. Whatever your AFTER THIS is, look for an open door to manifest, God to speak to you, and reveal to you what must be hereafter.

In the book of Matthew, Chapter 1, we find the genealogy of Christ. The scripture says in the book of Matthew 1:16-17, *"And Jacob begat Joseph the husband of Mary, of whom was born Jesus, who is called Christ. So all the generations from Abraham to David are fourteen generations; and from David until the carrying away into Babylon are fourteen generations; and from the carrying away into Babylon unto Christ are fourteen generations.*" The Spirit of the Lord revealed something to me that from Abraham to David there were 14 generations. Then from David was 14 generations and then to Christ was 14 generations. Remember, the number 14 represents complete deliverance and salvation for generations. But all of these generations were carried away into Babylon for verse 18, that says, *"....Now the birth!"* In earlier chapters, I told you that Babylon was known as "the place of confusion." So each generation was carried away into a "place of confusion" for the birth of a lifetime. Hear me clearly by the Spirit. This next birth will pierce the realm of darkness and speak with the enemy at the gate. There were many generations that went before you, but no one said "yes" to the birthing process for their life. However, when you said "yes", it was a "yes" that will bring with it restoration for generations. Your "yes" will birth a restoration of years. Your blood line is **barren no more** because you said "yes".

The afterbirth is the after the birth, after the warfare experience that a mother must go through or the process of labor is incomplete. What is God saying to you? The promise has been delivered, now the delivery of the afterbirth is required. What is the afterbirth in this chapter? In the book of Isaiah 66:10, the scripture says, *"Rejoice ye with Jerusalem, and be glad with her, all ye that love her."* The scripture say, REJOICE! In the book of Nehemiah, Chapter 12, Judah went first as the official to help Nehemiah in leading the celebration of the completion of the Jerusalem wall. **After** praise (Judah) went first, the scripture says in Nehemiah 12:32 that after them went Hoshaiah. Hoshaiah means "God saved." What point am I making? So **after** praise, God saved! Your praise is going to save you from many things in this season of the birthing process. I know we talked about Leah and her giving birth to Judah (praise) in an earlier chapter. However, you must build a wall of praise around your promise, build a wall of praise around the vision, and build a wall of praise around your business, your ministry, your children, and your marriage. Use your weapon of praise to build a wall and God will be their strong tower where the righteous run in and are safe!

The scripture says in the book of Isaiah 60:18-20, *"Violence shall no more be heard in thy land, wasting nor destruction within thy borders; but thou shalt call thy walls Salvation, and thy gates Praise. The sun shall be no more thy light by day; neither for brightness shall the moon give light unto thee: but the Lord shall be unto thee an everlasting light, and thy God thy glory. Thy sun shall no more go down; neither shall thy moon withdraw itself: for the Lord shall be thine everlasting light, and the days of thy mourning shall be ended."* The days of your mourning, your oppression, your doubt and all else will end if you build a wall of praise. Praise will eradicate the violence in your land and will ensure the security of the parameters around your family, home, job, ministry and all that is divinely connected to you. Therefore, choose to enter into His gates with thanksgiving and into His courts with praise! Because the moment you do, the Lord will set up a supernatural ambushment against your enemy (II Chronicles 20:15-22).

I decree and declare according to the book of Exodus 12:1-2, that this shall be the beginning of months for you. This day shall be the beginning of a new dawn, a new day, and the birthing of a new beginning. This day marks the beginning of your coming out! In the natural, before and after the baby comes out of a woman, water is released. The initial release of water is the breaking forth of waters. The scripture says in Micah 2:13, in the Amplified Bible, *"The Breaker [the Messiah] will go up before them. They will break through, pass in through the gate and go out through it, and their King will pass on before them, the Lord at their head."* Then the scripture says in I Chronicles 14:10-11, *"And David enquired of God, saying, Shall I go up against the Philistines? And wilt thou **deliver** them into mine hand? And the Lord said unto him, Go up; **for I will deliver them into thine hand**. So they came up to Baal-perazim; and David smote them there. Then David said, God hath broken in upon mine enemies by mine hand like the breaking forth of waters: therefore they called the name of that place Baal-perazim."* I see you at the place called Baal-perazim; the place of breakthrough. Do you see it? The Lord of the Breakthrough shall break in upon the head of your enemies as you praise Him and will deliver the release into your hands.

When the Lord breaks through, He will bring the rains! The rain, the former rain and the latter rain is coming through you (Joel 2:21-32). You may have been in a drought, but the time of the rains is right now! Unprecedented rains are coming. Sometimes after the birth, if the woman has a high leak, she may release more water. Look for the overflow. The type of overflow that the eyes have not seen and the ears have not heard (I

Corinthians 2:9-10).

There are many of you who for years have awaited a release such as this. Like the servant in I Kings, Chapter 18, you have said to God time and time again, "I don't see anything yet. It's been three years, five years or maybe even seven years and no return has manifested on what was planted." However, you didn't understand that the release or the afterbirth must be extracted by the midwife or the doctor. The doctor normally aids the removal of the afterbirth by gentling pulling it, but he must be careful not to exert any unnecessary traction, as it could tear the cord off. The umbilical cord must remain intact until it has been cut. I'll say that again, the umbilical cord must remain intact until it has been cut. After the birth, there are things that must be cut away for good. Your continual connection to the Word of God will ensure that those things that initially hindered your ability to birth will never attach to you again.

REFERENCES

Dr. Bree M. Keyton, T. D. (2002). Stripes, Nails, Thorns, and The Blood. In T. D. Dr. Bree M. Keyton, *Stripes, Nails, Thorns, and The Blood.* San Diego, California: Black Forest Press.

Gallup Management. (2001). Gallap Study Indicate Actively Disengaged Workders Cost U.S. Hundreds of Billions Each Year. *Gallup Management.*

M.R. DeHaan, M. (1943). The Chemistry of the Blood. In *The Chemistry of the Blood.* Grand Rapids, Michigan: Zondervan Publishing House.

Merriam-Webster. (2012). *Yoke.* Retrieved from Merriam-Webster Incorporated: http://www.merriam-webster.com/dictionary/yoke

Mize, J. (1993). Supernatural Childbirth. In J. Mize, *Supenatural Childbirth.* Tulsa, Oklahoma: Harrison House Inc.

Sullivan, D. (2011). *Why it Leads to Miscarriage. Why it Leads to Miscarriage- "Dr. Bryan Cowan".* Retrieved from Conceive: http://www.conceiveonline.com/articles/seven-most-common-miscarriage-causes

Tenney, T. (2003). Finding Favor with the King. In T. Tenney, *Finding Favor with the King.* Bloomington, Minnesota: Bethany House Productions.

Wikipedia. (2012, April 11). *Amniocentesis.* Retrieved from

Wikipedia- The Free Encyclopedia:
http://en.wikipedia.org/wiki/Amniocentesis

Zugibe, F. (2002). *Did Jesus Really Sweat Drops of Blood.* Retrieved from Christian Answers: http://www.christiananswers.net/q-eden/edn-t018.html

ACKNOWLEDGEMENTS

To my father, Edward Heard, may you rest in peace and my mother Betty J. Heard, who didn't abort the seed. Thank you for birthing me in the earth so that the birthing process could begin. I love you so much mommy!

To my grandmother, Mattie Heard, who picked me up every Saturday for our drive down Northside Drive in Atlanta, Georgia. Thank you Jesus for allowing her to lay hands on me at the age of 2 years old and prophesy me into my destiny. When the trumpet sounds……!

To my grandmother, Bessie L. Baker, who spoke my husband into existence. 17 years and counting. Oh, how I miss you "Nana"!....but again, when the trumpet sounds…!

To THE MAN AFTER GOD'S OWN HEART, my husband, Pastor Derek Howard…..you are truly the lifter up of my head. I so love you man of God!!!

To Keturah and Amariah…..if you can break through me….YOU GIRLS CAN BREAK THROUGH ANYTHING! Mommy loves you sooooo much!!

To Kia….what would I do without mommy's Kia. I guess I can't fire you now. The baby made it through the birth canal safely. YOU ARE THE GREATEST intercessor, assistant, minstrel, shopaholic…..Joe's Crab Shack-eater and all else. THANK YOU for traveling all around the world with me and laying down your life. God will openly reward you for your labor of love.

To my spiritual covering and "daddy", Apostle Bill Howard…Look at the fruit that is added to your account. Keep birthing us out daddy…God is well-pleased!

To my spiritual mommy, Apostle Judy Shaw….every prophesy has come to pass. I am grateful for the impact that you have made in my life. I will not stop until God has used me as a conduit to birth out all He desires.

To my sister, Kimberly Hughes, who I affectionately call "Judah", thank you for editing this "baby"….Judah's Writings Unlimited will forever be blessed.

To Liz, a.k.a."Gilead" a.k.a. "Condi" – thank you for obeying God by sowing your "Isaac" into our lives….you will forever reap! Love you girl!

To all my sisters who I know pray for me and have contributed to my birthing process: Prophetess Michelle Cade, Minister/CEO Sundra L Ryce, Pastor Sabrina "NFL", McKenzie, Pastor Felecia Bratton, Evangelist Desiree Sullivan, Bishop Sonnet Ford-Grant, Prophetess Marcelia Anderson, Apostle Lynnette Appling, Prophetess Debbie Coffman, Prophetess Mary Tiller Woods, Apostle Stacie Johnson, Evangelist Shelia Beavers, Lisa Culpepper, Prophetess Nia Fitzpatrick, Prophetess Francine Riley, Pastor Melanie Gleabes, Pastor Tanya Croone, First Lady Candee McKibbins, Dr. Pinky Miller, Sis. Perri Reid, Lady Lorna Roberts….each of you are oh so special! Love you!

To all my spiritual daughters…just remember, birth one "baby" at a time to alleviate frustration. However, don't just birth it, nourish it.

To every intercessor….you are the watchman that make the difference in the atmosphere. Thank you for your prayers.

To all those in the five-fold ministry who have allowed me to grace your pulpit and break the spirit of barrenness in your city, state, region and country....I love you immensely. We are truly a body that is fitly joined together.

www.ingramcontent.com/pod-product-compliance
Lightning Source LLC
Chambersburg PA
CBHW060108170426
43198CB00010B/817